ILLUSTRATED GUIDE TO
FAST PITCH
SOFTBALL

ILLUSTRATED GUIDE TO
FAST PITCH
SOFTBALL

By Brian Sobel

ANDERSON WORLD, INC.

Library of Congress Cataloging in Publication Data

Sobel, Brian, 1954 -
    The illustrated guide to fast pitch softball.

    1. Softball. I. Title.
GV881.S64   796.357'8   78-65624
ISBN 0-89037-173-3

Anderson World, Inc.
Mountain View, California

To my mom and dad, family, friends,
and Bonnie, the woman I love.

Contents

Preface

Across America and around the world, in small cities and sprawling metropolises, the game of softball is flourishing. Played now by almost thirty million Americans, it ranks as this nation's number one team participant sport. It exceeds football, baseball, basketball, soccer, hockey and many others combined! On the international scene, softball is played in more than fifty-five countries and on every continent of the planet.

The Amateur Softball Association, the main governing body in softball today, has almost twenty different tournament categories in which teams from all over the country compete. They range from the little known Men's Church Slow-Pitch tourney to the giant Men and Women's Major Fast-Pitch action which highlights the softball season.

In between, there are National Tournaments in almost every conceivable category. For example, there is the Women's Major Industrial Slow-Pitch, Men's "16-inch" Slow-Pitch, Girls ages 13-15 Fast-Pitch, Boys ages 16-18 Slow-Pitch and men's Major Slow-Pitch. These tourneys are what thousands of teams shoot for as they play softball each season around America.

The school systems have also recognized the value and versatility of softball. It is estimated that well over ninety percent of the junior high and high school programs in the fifty states play softball in their physical education classes. Many also sponsor after-school league competition.

The popularity of softball, in fact, is best illustrated by a statistic released by the ASA. It reported that team registrations in 1978 had topped the 100,000 mark for the first time in history. In contrast, the ASA had just 15,195 registered squads in 1964.

Many parts of the United States have reacted to the boom by building more softball diamonds. Few, however, touch the sheer grandeur of a complex appropriately named Softball City, in Detroit, Michigan. In what has to be one of the finest facilities in the world, the "city" is stretched over forty acres and has twelve fields, all fenced at 300 feet. It has lights, walkways, sunken dugouts, electronic scoreboards, concession stands and even a sporting goods shop selling the latest softball equipment. This complex, by the way, is the home field for some 1,620 slow-pitch teams!

In other parts of the country, fields and parks are being upgraded to accommodate the growing numbers wishing to compete. Many cities are running softball programs day and night just to keep up with the demand.

So a game that started in 1887 has come to be one of the most popular sports in the world, in less than a hundred years. Its unique history is one of my reasons for writing this book.

In addition, I hope that this book will be an instructional guide or manual for the fan, coach and player alike, as he or she works toward becoming more knowledgeable about and skilled in softball. I feel that the format used can best accomplish that goal. With the help of several nationally known fast-pitch players illustrating the art of softball through their own words and in pictures, hopefully we have achieved our aim.

For the fan, I offer the background of softball, particularly fast-pitch, that includes a concise history of the game, plus an easy-to-follow explanation of rules and strategies. The inexperienced player will benefit by gaining new insights on softball as these world class competitors give step-by-step instruction and advice on all aspects of the game.

For the coaches and veterans of many years, we think you will want to use this book in reviewing the game of softball.

I would like to acknowledge several people. Bill Fox, the man behind the camera for the invaluable camera sense in the stop-action world of sports photography. In addition, Mary Sobel provided the illustrations which aided us in the formation of this book.

The outstanding players who contributed their special knowledge of softball are also hereby thanked, as is the Amateur Softball Association for its kind assistance in the preparation of this book. Finally, I wish to express my deep appreciation for the help I received from Bill Cramer. Bill is the former coach and business manager of the world-famous Guanella Brothers softball team located in Santa Rosa, California. Bill has recently moved to Denver and will continue his association with softball there. His library of research materials on softball helped considerably, as did his personal knowledge of the game.

Also, as a point of reference, the players appearing in this book are also affiliated with Guanella's, except Ty Stofflet of the Hoffman York Barbell team in Leesport, Pennsylvania. Before changing sponsors at the beginning of the 1979 season, the team was called Billard Barbell. Billard with Ty at the helm won its second straight National Championship in 1978; its third championship in a four-year period.

In 1979, the Hoffman York Barbell team finished second in the ASA National Tournament behind McArdle Pontiac Cadillac of Midland, Michigan. Stofflet as mentioned earlier was selected first team All-American. Typical of past seasons, his pitching in 1979 was of exceptional caliber. Stofflet's pitching performances highlighted the softball portions of both the Pan-American games and the National Sports Festival. In addition, his 5-1 record at the ASA National Tournament ended what was a most successful year for Ty. His pitching tips are greatly appreciated.

We would be terribly remiss if we didn't mention the reading audience. Without your intense interest and widespread participation in softball, this game would have never attained the stature it now enjoys, and this book would not have been possible.

Introduction

The word "great" is an overused term in America's sports vernacular. It is invoked to describe so many players, no matter what the sport, that the adjective now draws little response. But when speaking of the players who have contributed to this volume, the word can accurately be applied. For all of the players without exception are of the highest caliber both on the field of play and in everyday life as well.

In each case the players in this book have competed at the highest levels of fast pitch softball. In that regard, they have excelled beyond the reach of most who ever play the game. They are the Rod Carews, Ron Guidrys, and Dave Parkers of their sport.

For these reasons, we feel especially fortunate that we have been able to call on five of the top players in fast pitch today. These people fit into the superior category nationally and have fine reputations throughout the United States. They are excellent representatives for the game of softball and are the type of players that are good for this game or any other.

We know you will enjoy their tips and insights, as this book delves into the different areas of softball as played by millions world wide.

A more formal introduction of the players begins with:

TY STOFFLET

The year was 1976 and Ty Stofflet was pitching for the United

States team in the World Softball Tournament being played in New Zealand. As if written in Hollywood, the finals matched the American team against the host New Zealand squad.

On that day, Ty Stofflet pitched himself into softball immortality with perhaps the most awesome performance in the history of the sport. Stofflet pitched a twenty inning no-hitter as the United States defeated New Zealand 1-0. In the 18th inning a player for the New Zealand squad reached first base, but not before Ty had coolly set down fifty-six batters in a row. By the game's completion, Stofflet had thrown to sixty-one batters, just one over the minimum, and struck out thirty-four. In addition, Ty knocked in the winning run.

For his efforts in winning four games in the World Tournament, Stofflet was named the most valuable pitcher and most valuable player in the tournament. It was the first time in history both awards were presented to the same person. The Tourney was unfortunately rained out and the United States, New Zealand and Canada were proclaimed tri-champions. About his famous game Stofflet recalls, "I had 18-2/3 perfect innings going before a guy stepped over the plate and I nicked him on the arm, sending him to first base. It didn't matter; I was feeling great. I felt so super it was unbelievable. Every pitch was working and going my way."

Needless to say, Ty considers that game his greatest thrill in softball. However, his many fans in softball circles can recall a separate performance of softball prowess exhibited by this fabulous pitcher. Many speak of games in which it seemed as if no one in the world was capable of laying a bat on the pitches of Ty Stofflet.

Some of his finest accolades come from the players who have faced him in recent seasons. K. G. Fincher, also one of the best pitchers in the history of the game, says of Stofflet, "Right now, there is nobody better. In fact, he's head and shoulders above anyone else in the game. There is nobody in the same class with Ty Stofflet."

Ray Allena says, "He is the only guy I've ever seen pitch who does not ever have a bad game. He'll throw any pitch to any batter; he has that much confidence. He's thrown a couple of pitches to me I don't think I saw."

Stofflet has played on several National Championship teams,

Ty Stofflet is shown here during a game in preparation for the 1979 Pan American games. Notice the fierce determination and power Ty exhibits as he releases the ball. (This picture was taken by George Wilson of the *Oklahoma-Journal* and used with the permission of the ASA.)

most recently with the Billard Barbell squad from Reading, Pennsylvania. Now in his late thirties, he appears to be reaching his prime. Ty's 1978 statistics bear this out. He was 46-1, with his only loss to Home Savings and Loan of Aurora, Illinois. His setback broke a seventy-one game winning streak over two seasons. He threw twenty-six shutouts, and in 334 innings struck out 641 batters. In 1978 he allowed only twenty-four earned runs for an 0.67 earned run average. Stofflet tossed five no-hitters over the course of the season, including one in the opening game of the national tournament.

Stofflet started pitching softball at the age of twelve. "My father," says Stofflet, "was a softball pitcher and he coached me along. We worked day in and day out in the back yard, mostly on control. He taught me enough at that age to make me look like I knew what I was doing."

At age sixteen Stofflet started pitching in the Church league. Four years later the lefthander joined a team from Allentown, Pennsylvania. He played on that team for almost eight years.

In 1968, a club called Sal's Lunch, based in Philadelphia, Pennsylvania, asked Stofflet to play for them. Ty decided he would, and in 1969 this team won the International Softball Congress World Championship.

In 1970 Ty was with the Rising Sun team of Reading, Pennsylvania. That team changed its name to Billard Barbell. Now with his present team, Stofflet has shown the skills that make him one of the best pitchers ever to play softball.

K. G. FINCHER

Every now and again in sports a player at a certain position will have the ability to dominate opposing teams over a number of years. In baseball or softball it can be a pitcher for example. Ty Stofflet and the great Herb Dudley of Clearwater, Florida have both done so at that position.

For K. G. Fincher, that kind of domination has also been his trademark since 1952 when he first picked up a ball to pitch. Since that time K. G. has won as many or more important games than almost anyone in softball history. Like Stofflet, Fincher has thoroughly controlled the opposition for most of his career.

The highlights in Fincher's long career in softball are almost too numerous to list. Some, like his pitching fifty-seven innings in one day, as his team won four games and lost one, stick out. Or the twenty-two-inning game he once pitched and won is also a highlight. Another standout performance was his winning all five games for the Gardena, California Merchants in the 1966 ISC Championships held in Rock Island, Illinois. K. G.'s pitching also contributed greatly to the Guanella Brothers ASA National Championship in 1974. And the list goes on and on. In addition, Fincher has been on several other national title winning teams in both ISC and ASA competition.

Like Stofflet, Fincher started in the Church leagues, beginning in his junior year in high school in 1952. He competed for five years in the Church league before joining a tournament team. Fincher remembers, "I got to play with a team from Escondido, California, in the ISC league. We played all over. Our team had two other pitchers besides myself. The year before these two had combined to go thirty-five innings in a World Tournament game. Anyway, I didn't get to play much because, as the manager said, I had the tools, but lacked the confidence."

The next season Fincher found himself as the only pitcher on the club. The other two had not returned to play with Escondido. That was a large factor in the success of K. G. Fincher, for he pitched the whole season by himself and the team ended the year by finishing third in the state tournament.

About the following season, Fincher says, "I turned down the Long Beach Nitehawks, one of the best teams going, and instead played softball for the Gardena, California Merchants." He played on the Merchants for four seasons out of the next five. In that time Fincher established himself as one of the best pitchers in softball. In addition to pitching almost 100 games a season, he led them to the 1963 ISC championship and a repeat as champions in 1966.

K. G. had left in 1965 to play for a team in Rock Island, Illinois. He, however, considered that a one-year opportunity, and returned to the West Coast.

The 1966 season was one of Fincher's finest. "The year I returned from Illinois, the Merchants had a fair start and then really came alive in the state tournament," recalls K. G. "The winner of that tournament would then go back to the ISC world championships. On the last night of the state tournament we had to beat an undefeated team twice, which we did to win the tourney. I pitched both games which went eleven innings apiece, and were won by identical 1-0 scores."

"We went to the world tournament and I threw four of the five games and didn't give up a run. The one game I did not start, I came in and finished. In that game we scored a late inning run and I got the win!" Fincher ended the world tourney with a 5-0 record as the Merchants won the ISC championship. Incredible as it may seem, he did not give up a run and was voted the most valuable player of the series.

Before playing for the Guanella Brothers team in Santa Rosa, California, Fincher pitched for teams from San Diego to Sunnyvale, California and did well for all. In those years he pitched in several national championship tournaments. Along the way, K.G. even pitched in a newly formed professional softball league.

Signing and then pitching for a team located in Mobile, Alabama, he played one weekend of pro ball before the league folded. For his effort he did not receive a penny and therefore was allowed to keep his amateur status. Fincher played out the year pitching once again in the amateur ranks.

"In 1974, I decided to play for the Guanella Brothers of Santa Rosa," remarks K.G. "That team fell together perfectly and thanks to great influx of talent went on to win the ASA national title."

Since that time he has played for Guanella's every season except 1977. That year he elected to pitch for the Super Auto team from Napa, California. Napa, not far from Santa Rosa, had many of the former Guanella's players on their roster that season. However, most of the major players did return to Santa Rosa in time to start the following year of softball.

So over the years since 1952, K.G. Fincher has been a dominating force in softball. Winning National and World titles in both the ASA and ISC, he has without a doubt established himself as one of the top pitchers in the history of softball.

RAY ALLENA

Some teams search and may never locate a player who can be both consistent at the plate and possess the ability to hit the long ball. Match that offensive prowess with great defensive skills and one will see quickly why Ray Allena is perhaps the best all-around player in the game today.

After having played baseball through high school and junior college, Ray decided to shift his emphasis and concentrate on playing big-time softball. In 1973, he made the move after a period in which he was playing hardball, softball and lob-ball over ten times a week.

Allena can remember his early days in softball, playing with friends from his hometown of Petaluma, California. "I'll never forget a game early in my first season in which I went to the plate four times," says Allena. "I took twelve swings and never touched the ball. I went away talking to myself."

After making the decision to concentrate on softball exclusively, Ray was asked to join a team called Wilson-Russell from Vallejo, California. He remembers, "It was 1973 and I was having second thoughts because it was so structured. I didn't know if I wanted to make the kind of commitment it would take to become good. But my father told me at the time that if I ever wanted to go somewhere in softball I'd better get started. At that point, I began working hard on the game."

Ray, upon his father's advice, joined Wilson-Russell and had a fair season. It was a new experience for Allena because the competition was of such high caliber. As 1974 rolled around, he decided to join Guanella's. Allena was a major part of the influx of talent which K. G. Fincher referred to earlier. With Allena having a great year at the plate, the 1974 team went on to win the ASA National Championship.

In 1974, Allena gave an indication of what he was to become in softball. Ray hit for a .426 average with twenty-one home runs, twenty-three triples and twenty-nine doubles. After just two seasons in big-time softball, that is quite some accomplishment for any player.

Allena has since become a main cog in the Guanella Brothers machine. Softball observers agree that Ray is one of the best playing the sport at this time. And if past performance is an indicator we will likely see his tremendous hitting and fielding continue for some time to come.

MIKE PARNOW

Mike Parnow, nicknamed "Whitey," is called by teammate K. G. Fincher "the best all around third baseman in America." In addition says Fincher, "Mike is a great glove at third, plus he's so quick it can only help."

Parnow is another of the relative newcomers to softball who

will see many years of high caliber softball. After being released from the Los Angeles Dodgers system minor league, Parnow started playing fast-pitch softball. "I got started in 1974," comments Mike. "I played for a team called Suburban Auto out of Marin County, California." In 1976, Mike started playing for another Marin County team called Marin Wheel Alignment. The Wheel was playing good teams at the time, but halfway through the season, Parnow started going to high caliber tournaments with Guanella's. Parnow ended that season playing full time with the Guanella Brothers team.

Mike has been with Guanella's since. He said Guanella's is "like night and day from any team I've ever been on. All they think about is winning. It is quite enjoyable. Everyone respects each other and there is a genuine good feeling among the players."

Parnow has also become widely known for his ability to make the super play at third base. In addition, his batting has improved with each season. The future looks good for Mike Parnow, for he is a ballplayer who is always attempting to better himself at the plate and in the field. The enthusiasm and love for the game of softball exhibited by him both on and off the field, plus his outstanding abilities, mark him as one of the stars in softball today.

JIM MARSH

Jim Marsh began playing softball at the "B" level, in 1975. "B" league softball is played by a cross-section of athletes. Some are players coming up from the "C" leagues and pointing to the "A" competition. For others it may be where they feel most comfortable in playing. However, the rapid improvement shown by Marsh in going from the "B" leagues to top level softball has surprised many who believe it takes several years to play at that level successfully.

Drafted and subsequently released by the Oakland Athletics organization, Marsh has adjusted well to the game of softball after years of playing baseball.

Following the year of "B" league ball, Marsh played two years of major fast-pitch softball before joining Super Auto of Napa, California in 1977. That season Jim gained valuable experience by playing for a superior team that ended the year by traveling to the ASA National Tournament and doing very well.

Marsh played the 1978 season in Santa Rosa, playing for Guanella's, and says about softball, "I actually got to top softball very quickly—two years and I was here. I've been very fortunate. It, to me, is a better game than baseball. I played baseball from little league on up, including three-and-a-half years of minor league ball, and find I enjoy this game much more."

As for the catcher's position, Marsh says, "I like catching. It's a position where I feel a part of the action no matter where the ball is on the diamond."

Barring injuries and other problems that can plague a catcher over a period of years, one may expect to see Jim Marsh playing softball for seasons to come.

1

History of Softball

Like most sports, the game of softball has its unique beginnings. Although a touch clouded by the passage of time, the story of softball in the beginning years has remained substantially the same. For whatever reasons, these years have not undergone the intense scrutiny that often accrues to a sport's embarkation period. It would be a safe bet to say that very few people know the origin of softball. However, common sense tells us that it must have been influenced by baseball to a large degree, and that is where this account begins.

In 1887, America was led by Grover Cleveland, the twenty-second President of the United States and a Democrat with years of service in the state of New York. Cleveland had won the election to the Presidency in 1884 by the slimmest of margins, with 219 electoral votes to Republican James G. Blaine's 182.

In point of time it was just twenty-two years after the Civil War and eleven years since America's Grand Centennial. Six years before in 1881, Charles Guiteau had assassinated President James A. Garfield. America was in the age of steel and steam, with railroads fast becoming the only viable means of comfortable transcontinental travel.

It was an age of invention. In 1875, Alexander Graham Bell had invented the telephone, and in 1892 Bell made the first New York-to-Chicago phone call. In 1879 the electric light was invented by Thomas Edison. Other notable items such as the camera and telegraph were improved immensely.

America was expanding into the West, and along with the people came technology to bind the nation coast-to-coast in every possible way. In short, America was a very busy nation. As Cleveland was minding the country's official business, the country at its leisure was proceeding to make baseball the national sport.

Some years before, in 1845 the Knickerbocker Base Ball Club of New York was formed by a group of well-to-do fellows in that city.

The club was perhaps the first real baseball team in America. The rules for the game played by those sportsmen were written by a team member named Alexander Cartwright. Cartwright was a civil engineer by trade and a part time ballplayer. He had developed rules to set his game apart from any other and to assure standardized play.

The Knickerbocker team played their first game on June 19, 1846. In a contest that lasted four innings the Knickerbockers lost to a team called the New York Nine 23-1.

Also around the same time period, one Abner Doubleday was receiving credit for inventing the game of baseball as we know it today. The actual inventor of baseball was a dispute that lasted many years. However, before that complex point was resolved the game grew beyond anyones expectations.

Several factors contributed to the spread of baseball. One major element was the Civil War. Troops from both the North and South played the sport in various camps and posts. They in turn taught it to those who had never played. Following the war, soldiers returned home and formed teams and leagues. In 1867, there was a baseball convention that brought delegates in from 237 teams located in eight states. Also in 1867, a club called the Washington Nationals made the first country-wide tour.

The formation of professional teams quickened the expansion of baseball and tended to give it a solid unity. When the various professional teams banded together in 1871, they formed a league called the National Association of Professional Baseball Players. That league lasted five seasons and was followed in 1876 by the National League which exists to this day.

By the late 1870s, Americans in large numbers were playing

baseball and enjoying it more than any other sport. It combined skill, hard work, and hustle—the ingredients that made the young Republic strong.

In any case, baseball had become so popular by the turn of the century that in 1908 a commission was formed to determine how baseball had begun and who was to receive credit for inventing the sport. The commission was appointed by A.G. Spalding, head of the now-famous sporting goods company, and was composed of three former presidents of the National League.

The commission concluded that Abner Doubleday was the sole inventor of baseball and further, that baseball was an American game with no "foreign" origins.

The "no foreign origin" theory has since been refuted many times. The actual origins of baseball can be traced back to an English game called rounders. That game was described in a text published in 1828 called *The Boy's Own Book*, as one that was played on a diamond with bases at the four corners.

A batter would hit the ball and run. If he touched all four bases, then his side was awarded a point. If the batter hit a ball that was caught on the fly, he was out. He was also judged out if he missed three pitches in one time at bat. The rules also provided for fair and foul balls, such as in the American version of baseball. One of the only significant differences between the two games is that in rounders, one could get a runner out by fielding a batted ball and throwing it at the batter, hitting him somewhere on the body. No such rule exists in American baseball.

So the American game of baseball, with its origins in England is, in effect, the child of rounders, which makes softball the grandchild, as we will plainly see.

Although two men are frequently mentioned together concerning the invention of softball, one stands out as the "father" of the game. His name is George Hancock. Hancock, along with another fellow named Lewis Rober, were, in the period between 1885 and 1887, given local credit for inventing softball.

Rober was a fireman in Minneapolis, Minnesota. Along about the same time as Hancock, the fireman started thinking about an indoor-outdoor baseball game. Years later he was the person cited in Minnesota as the one who conceived the sport. Little is known about Rober, and down through the years very little has been mentioned about him in softball circles. For that reason he has drifted somewhat into obscurity.

Hancock, on the other hand, was the recipient of more print publicity, both then and now. There is no question who had the larger influence on the development of softball. That honor goes to Hancock. He was without question the first person to devise rules and form a structure the game could use in its formative years.

It was a late afternoon near the end of November in Chicago, Illinois. The year was 1887 and a typical winter had forced even the brave to seek shelter. As darkness was settling over the Farragut Boat Club, George Hancock was mulling over a new game.

He took an old beat-up boxing glove and formed it into a ball and tied it to stay. Then he grabbed a broomstick and gave it to another person in the gym. We can only suppose that these two hit the ball around until it caught the interest of the others in the building. In any case, within a short period of time Hancock had everyone formed into teams and the rest of that day was spent experimenting with the new-found sport. Hancock was so excited that he went home that night and set on paper an entire set of rules.

As the next Saturday came, Hancock was to be found in the gym explaining his new concept to those present. Besides the new rules, he had developed a better ball and had fashioned a softball bat.

From that time on, every weekend during the winter, players competed in softball at Farragut's gym. The contests soon featured cloth bags and a diamond painted on the gym floor. That was just the beginning. Soon people all over Chicago were playing the new game, and from that point a rapid development began taking place with rising numbers of people participating.

As the winter of 1887 drew to a close and people would no longer stay indoors in favor of spring and summer, the game moved outside and proved equally popular. Since the name softball had not yet been coined, the sport instead was called indoor-outdoor.

Meanwhile, baseball was sweeping the country. More and more people were beginning to play it as well as the various forms of softball. Hancock was probably the first, but by no means the only person to ponder a more competitive sport for all. Softball was a slower and more exciting game for the masses, and it was finding popularity around the country while going by different names and rules in different regions. All this, just a few years after Hancock had started playing his game in Chicago.

Indoor-outdoor, beyond Illinois and in Canada, was variously known as diamond ball, mush ball, kitten ball, recreation ball, fast ball and many other names. Up until 1933, almost every portion of the country had a different set of rules. In addition, no two balls were the same size nor the dimensions of the fields anywhere close to one another, be that across town or across country.

The confusing situation in softball was epitomized by the National Diamond Ball Association when they invited forty teams to a tournament. The forty teams were to be worthy representatives of softball in different sections of the United States. Much to everyone's amazement and chagrin, all forty teams came bearing a different set of rules.

In the early Thirties, many softball league administrators began to recognize the need for uniformity and through the energies of a man named Leo Fisher began to work together to create what was to become known as the Amateur Softball Association. Fisher had been primarily responsible for a national tournament in 1933 which proved highly successful. After the conclusion of that tourney, the visitors got together and drew up a uniform set of rules to put softball on an organized track.

Fisher was named the ASA's first president and served in that capacity until 1939, when he retired. It is clear that without the likes of George Hancock, Lewis Rober, Leo Fisher and several other pioneers, this game would not have developed to the degree that it has.

The ASA today is led by Don Porter. Porter has served that organization for many years and is a most capable representative of amateur softball, not only in the United States, but around the world.

From it's earliest days, softball has been played by American servicemen stationed overseas. Primarily because of that, the game became so popular around the world that many countries have instituted national softball programs. The ASA is affiliated with the International Softball Federation, an organization that lists forty-three countries around the world as members. When it comes to this country's involvement in softball, Don Porter finds himself a very busy man.

Worldwide play in softball started in 1965. In that year the first global tournament was held in Melbourne, Australia, pitting the world's best women's teams against one another. Team Australia thrilled the home country fans by defeating the United States team, 1-0, in the final game to win the world crown.

In 1966, the men staged their first World Tournament in Mexico City. The American team proved awesome and completed a clean sweep, winning ten straight games and capturing the championship. Softball observers are now predicting that the sport will be included very soon in the Olympic program. Already the game is being played on a worldwide basis in the Pan-American, Asian and Central American-Caribbean games. It would, of course, be another large step in softball history to compete in the Olympics.

Recently, another organization in the United States has started to gain prominence in softball circles. The International Softball Congress (ISC) is much like the ASA in its constitution, and has been staging tournaments since 1958. In that year the ISC merged with the National Softball Congress. The NSC had been holding national tourneys since 1947. For those interested, both associations have Halls of Fame. The ASA hall is located in Oklahoma City, Oklahoma, and the ISC hall is in Long Beach, California.

How the game of softball progresses from this point on is really anybody's guess, but its development has been a fast-paced one involving many dedicated people who have served to help the game grow to what it is today.

Below is a listing of ASA National Champions since 1933. In both the men's and women's ranks you will see repeat winners. Absolute dominance in any sport is unusual, but when it comes to softball, there are several teams that have established this pattern. In the women's fast-pitch ranks, the Raybestos Brakettes of Stratford, Connecticut, stand out as the all-time perennial champ. In 1978, they won their eighth national Championship in a row, a feat of enormous proportions. From 1933 to 1978 the Brakettes won the National Championship fifteen times!

In addition to the Raybestos Brakettes, two other teams have also had many championship seasons. One is the Orange Lionettes from Orange, California, who have tasted victory nine times since their first National win in 1950. The other is the Jax Maids, based in New Orleans, Louisiana. The Maids won the national title five times in the six seasons between 1942 and 1947.

On the men's side, perhaps the finest all-time team is the Clearwater Bombers from Clearwater, Florida. Since 1933 the Bombers have captured ten national titles. The name Raybestos appears again, this time on the men's side as the Raybestos Cardinals, also from Stratford, Connecticut. The Cardinals have captured the national title four times since their first United States championship in 1955.

NATIONAL WOMEN'S FAST-PITCH SOFTBALL CHAMPIONS

YEAR	PLACE	CHAMPIONS
1933	Chicago, Ill.	Great Northerns, Chicago, Ill.
1934	Chicago, Ill.	Hart Motors, Chicago, Ill.
1935	Chicago, Ill.	Bloomer Girls, Cleveland, Ohio
1936	Chicago, Ill.	National Mfg. Co., Cleveland, Ohio
1937	Chicago, Ill.	National Mfg. Co., Cleveland, Ohio
1938	Chicago, Ill.	J. J. Kreig's, Alameda, Calif.
1939	Chicago, Ill.	J. J. Kreig's, Alameda, Calif.
1940	Detroit, Mich.	Arizona Ramblers, Phoenix, Ariz.
1941	Detroit, Mich.	Higgins "Midgets", Tulsa, Okla.
1942	Detroit, Mich.	Jax Maids, New Orleans, La.
1943	Detroit, Mich.	Jax Maids, New Orleans, La.
1944	Cleveland, Ohio	Lind & Pomeroy, Portland, Ore.
1945	Cleveland, Ohio	Jax Maids, New Orleans, La.
1946	Cleveland, Ohio	Jax Maids, New Orleans, La.
1947	Cleveland, Ohio	Jax Maids, New Orleans, La.
1948	Portland, Ore.	Arizona Ramblers, Phoenix, Ariz.
1949	Portland, Ore.	Arizona Ramblers, Phoenix, Ariz.
1950	San Antonio, Texas	Orange Lionettes, Orange, Calif.
1951	Detroit, Mich.	Orange Lionettes, Orange, Calif.
1952	Toronto, Can.	Orange Lionettes, Orange, Calif.
1953	Toronto, Can.	Betsy Ross Rockets, Fresno, Calif.
1954	Orange, Calif.	Leach Motor Rockets, Fresno, Calif.
1955	Portland, Ore.	Orange Lionettes, Orange, Calif.
1956	Clearwater, Fla.	Orange Lionettes, Orange, Calif.

1957	Buena Park, Calif.	Betsy Ross Rockets, Fresno, Calif.
1958	Stratford, Conn.	Raybestos Brakettes, Stratford, Conn.
1959	Stratford, Conn.	Raybestos Brakettes, Stratford, Conn.
1960	Stratford, Conn.	Raybestos Brakettes, Stratford, Conn.
1961	Portland, Ore.	Gold Sox, Whittier, Calif.
1962	Stratford, Conn.	Orange Lionettes, Orange, Calif.
1963	Stratford, Conn.	Raybestos Brakettes, Stratford, Conn.
1964	Orlando, Fla.	Erv Lind Florists, Portland, Ore.
1965	Stratford, Conn.	Orange Lionettes, Orange, Calif.
1966	Orlando, Fla.	Raybestos Brakettes, Stratford, Conn.
1967	Stratford, Conn.	Raybestos Brakettes, Stratford, Conn.
1968	Stratford, Conn.	Raybestos Brakettes, Stratford, Conn.
1969	Tucson, Ariz.	Orange Lionettes, Orange, Calif.
1970	Stratford, Conn.	Orange Lionettes, Orange, Calif.
1971	Orlando, Fla.	Raybestos Brakettes, Stratford, Conn.
1972	Tucson, Ariz.	Raybestos Brakettes, Stratford, Conn.
1973	Stratford, Conn.	Raybestos Brakettes, Stratford, Conn.
1974	Orlando, Fla.	Raybestos Brakettes, Stratford, Conn.
1975	Salt Lake City, Utah	Raybestos Brakettes, Stratford, Conn.
1976	Stratford, Conn.	Raybestos Brakettes, Stratford, Conn.
1977	Hayward, Calif.	Raybestos Brakettes, Stratford, Conn.
1978	Allentown, Pa.	Raybestos Brakettes, Stratford, Conn.
1979	Springfield, Mo.	Sun City Saints, Sun City, Ariz.

NATIONAL MEN'S FAST-PITCH SOFTBALL CHAMPIONS

YEAR	PLACE	CHAMPIONS
1933	Chicago, Ill.	J. J. Giths, Chicago, Ill.
1934	Chicago, Ill.	KeNash-A's, Kenosha, Wis.
1935	Chicago, Ill.	Crimson Coaches, Toledo, Ohio
1936	Chicago, Ill.	Kodak Park, Rochester, N. Y.
1937	Chicago, Ill.	Briggs Mfg. Co., Detroit, Mich.
1938	Chicago, Ill.	Pohlers, Cincinnati, Ohio
1939	Chicago, Ill.	Carr's, Covington, Ky.
1940	Detroit, Mich.	Kodak Park, Rochester, N.Y.
1941	Detroit, Mich.	Bendix Brakes, South Bend, Ind.
1942	Detroit, Mich.	Deep Rock Oilers, Tulsa, Okla.
1943	Detroit, Mich.	Hammer Field, Fresno, Calif.
1944	Cleveland, Ohio	Hammer Field, Fresno, Calif.
1945	Cleveland, Ohio	Zollner's Pistons, Ft. Wayne, Ind.
1946	Cleveland, Ohio	Zollner's Pistons, Ft. Wayne, Ind.
1947	Cleveland, Ohio	Zollner's Pistons, Ft. Wayne, Ind.
1948	Portland, Ore.	Briggs Beautyware, Detroit, Mich.
1949	Little Rock, Ark.	Tip-Top Clothiers, Toronto, Can.
1950	Austin, Texas	Clearwater Bombers, Clearwater, Fla.

1951	Detroit, Mich.	Dow Chemical Co., Midland, Mich.
1952	Stratford, Conn.	Briggs Beautyware, Detroit, Mich.
1953	Miami, Fla.	Briggs Beautyware, Detroit, Mich.
1954	Minneapolis, Minn.	Clearwater Bombers, Clearwater, Fla.
1955	Clearwater, Fla.	Raybestos, Stratford, Conn.
1956	Sacramento, Calif.	Clearwater Bombers, Clearwater, Fla.
1957	Clearwater, Fla.	Clearwater Bombers, Clearwater, Fla.
1958	Minneapolis, Minn.	Raybestos, Stratford, Conn.
1959	Clearwater, Fla.	Sealmasters, Aurora, Ill.
1960	Long Island, N.Y.	Clearwater Bombers, Clearwater, Fla.
1961	Clearwater, Fla.	Sealmasters, Aurora, Ill.
1962	Stratford, Conn.	Clearwater Bombers, Clearwater, Fla.
1963	Clearwater, Fla.	Clearwater Bombers, Clearwater, Fla.
1964	Sunnyvale, Calif.	Burch Tool, Detroit, Mich.
1965	Clearwater, Fla.	Sealmasters, Aurora, Ill.
1966	Indianapolis, Ind.	Clearwater Bombers, Clearwater, Fla.
1967	Springfield, Mo.	Sealmasters, Aurora, Ill.
1968	Clearwater, Fla.	Clearwater Bombers, Clearwater, Fla.
1969	Springfield, Mo.	Raybestos Cardinals, Stratford, Conn.
1970	Clearwater, Fla.	Raybestos Cardinals, Stratford, Conn.
1971	Springfield, Mo.	Welty Way, Cedar Rapids, Iowa
1972	Dallas, Texas	Raybestos Cardinals, Stratford, Conn.
1973	Seattle, Wash.	Clearwater Bombers, Clearwater, Fla.
1974	Clearwater, Fla.	Guanella Bros., Santa Rosa, Calif.
1975	Hayward, Calif.	Rising Sun Motel, Reading, Pa.
1976	Allentown, Pa.	Raybestos Cardinals, Stratford, Conn.
1977	Midland, Mich.	Billard Barbell, Reading, Pa.
1978	Springfield, Mo.	Billard Barbell, Reading, Pa.
1979	Midland, Mich.	McArdle Pontiac Cadillac, Midland, Mich.

2

Equipment

One of the reasons softball has achieved such widespread popularity is that it takes a bare minimum of equipment to play. The equipment factor has always been the common bond between the school systems and your average Sunday-in-the-park player. In many schools around the United States and world only a few gloves are available on a first come, first served basis. The rest must use their bare hands. The same is true for numerous pick-up games in the park. A group of people can get together and play in much the same fashion as did their early forebears around Chicago in the late 1800s.

Simply stated, one needs only two items to begin a softball game—bat and a ball, no more and no less. From there the equipment can grow in volume and sophistication until it reaches the level of big-time softball competition. These teams of course utilize the modern bats, gloves, catcher's gear and all the rest, and can be counted on to dress in the very latest uniform styles.

Although only a handful of people ever get to play the caliber of softball seen at national tournaments, we can assume for the purposes of this book that few games nowadays are contested with only bare hands, a bat and ball; more likely some combination of the equipment mentioned is used. Keeping that in mind, it is advisable to obtain basic gear which conforms with the safety and rule requirements of softball.

This is some of the equipment used in a softball game. Included are bats, ball, glove and "donut" which adds weight to the bat when swinging in the on-deck circle.

The official rulebook, as adopted by the International Joint Rules Committee on Softball, describes equipment under Rule Three, Sections One through Ten. It includes the official measurements and construction of home plate, pitcher's mound, and the bases. Also covered are the gloves, mitts, shoes, masks, and uniforms that players wear.

Section Nine of Rule Three states that no equipment should be left lying on the field, either in fair or foul territory. Anyone who has ever dodged equipment strewn on a playing field while attempting to catch a fly ball knows why this rule exists. A more in-depth look at equipment starts with the bats used in softball and continues through the players official dress code.

BATS

The softball bat, according to the rules, shall be round, made of one piece of hard wood, or formed from a block of wood consisting of two or more pieces of wood bonded together with an adhesive, in such a way that the grain direction of all pieces is essentially parallel to the length of the bat. Plastic and bamboo substances are also deemed acceptable under the rules.

It is also specified that the bat will not exceed thirty-four inches in length, nor two and one-quarter inches in diameter at the bat's largest section. In addition, the bat cannot exceed thirty-eight ounces in total weight.

Bats may also be made of metal. For that reason, aluminum bats have become extremely popular throughout the United States. Most fast-pitch teams use these bats and find them to their liking. All bats, whether made of wood, aluminum or other acceptable substance, must be stamped with the words, "OFFICIAL SOFTBALL" by the manufacturer before they can be used in league or tournament play.

BALLS

In the early days of softball, almost every league had a different size ball. Some differences were quite large. In many cases the variation was like that between an orange and a grapefruit.

No longer is that the case. Today's official softball must be no smaller than 11-7/8 inches, or larger than 12-1/8 inches in circumference.

There are also other specifications the ball must meet in the way it is constructed. All of these guidelines seek to insure that every league uses a softball similar in size and composition. The only variations one might see are that some balls have a restricted flight capability. Balls of this type are built to go a shorter distance than those normally used in softball. Many slow-pitch leagues use a restricted flight ball in regular season play. Other variations from the regular softball in use today are ones with a rubber coating and those balls with a bright yellow or bright white covering for night use. In addition a sixteen inch ball is sometimes

Gloves come in all sizes and shapes. Be sure to pick one that best suits your hand and position on the field.

used in slow-pitch, depending on the league. The use of this ball is covered by separate rules.

GLOVES AND MITTS

Gloves and mitts are defined differently in the rules of softball. The glove which is five-fingered may be worn by any player on the field. But a mitt which does not have individual slots for each finger may be worn only by the first baseman and catcher.

The rules also stipulate that a pitcher's glove may be only one solid color other than gray or white, and will have no marking on the outside that may resemble a softball.

Gloves today are made in all price ranges and vary in quality accordingly. It is a good idea, therefore, to consult other members of your team or organization before purchasing a glove or mitt. This will help you determine which brands are doing the job over the course of a season. Above all remember to select your glove very carefully. It is one of the most personal pieces of equipment a player uses.

SHOES

In the past few years baseball and softball shoes, which are primarily the same, have improved both in adaptability and appearance. Officially speaking, shoes are legal for softball if the shoe upper in question has been made of leather, canvas or similar materials. In addition, the spikes on the shoe may not exceed three-quarters of an inch. It is also stated that soles with smooth, soft or hard cleats may be used.

While on the subject of shoes, we should mention that a pitcher who sees considerable action needs what is known as a pitcher's toe or plate. The toe is a heavy leather or metal addition to the existing shoe, which helps protect it from intense wear and tear. This deterioration of a pitcher's shoe results from dragging the back foot across the ground as the pitch is released.

UNIFORMS

Softball and baseball uniforms have changed considerably as the games themselves have evolved. Once the game was played in baggy pants and shirts that lacked both color and personality.

Mike Parnow on the left and Ray Allena on the right model the uniforms used in softball today. Many teams have several sets of uniforms with style changes in each.

Now the uniforms range from tight-fitting models to the almost skin-tight double knit versions. In most cases, today's uniforms explode in color and are comfortable to wear. It is a rule, however, that all players on the same team must wear the same style uniform; one that is identical in color, trim and design style. The rules strictly prohibit torn or ragged undershirts which are exposed to view. This also applies to the use of a torn or frayed uniform during the game.

OTHER EQUIPMENT

As an adjunct to the equipment previously mentioned, other items are necessary. For a team, one would want a first aid kit, bat and ball bags, plus a scorebook. In the personal sense, a player should always carry and use his own glove and shoes, both of which need to be given close attention at all times. There is nothing worse than getting ready prior to a game and having a shoelace break, or playing catch before the batter steps to the

(Left) Jim Marsh is shown here in catcher's gear. A fast-pitch catcher would be wise to wear at least this much equipment when playing. (Right) K. G. Fincher wearing a newly introduced arm warmer. This allows a pitcher to keep the arm heated without wearing a full jacket.

Jim Marsh demonstrates the proper way to put on shin guards.

plate and having the glove lacing snap. Many times this can be avoided by keeping equipment in the best of shape.

After all, proper equipment does not make the man or woman. But it sure can help where the batting average and fielding percentage is concerned!

3

Field Layout and Rules

As softball was developing, but before the ASA established rules and field dimensions, the game lacked any real unity. All across the country thousands of people were playing forms of softball on fields of different sizes and configurations. Getting all the leagues in the United States to use one standard set of rules proved to be a long and monumental task. Equally as difficult was the setting of dimensions for a suitable field layout.

Although the rules have undergone some changes since that original version, the game itself remains essentially unchanged. The official softball rules cover about everything one needs to know about softball. Some of the items included are the regulation pitching and fence distances for men and women's fast-pitch and slow-pitch softball, as well as the dimensions for everything on the field, from coaches' boxes to the on-deck circle.

The regulations list almost every conceivable situation that can arise on a softball field and what the official position is on the occurrence in question. Also incorporated in the International Joint Rules Committee books are the sixteen-inch rules, which refer to the regulations governing the slow-pitch game of softball that uses a sixteen-inch ball. The International Joint Rules Committee is an organization that attempts to keep softball played the same around the world by adopting rules on an international basis.

The actual playing field must, according to standards, be an

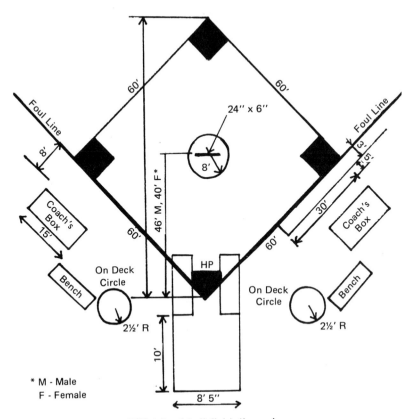

Official softball field dimensions.

area that is clear and unobstructed within a radius of 225 feet or 74.25 meters between the foul lines and extending from home plate to the outfield fence. The area outside the foul lines and reaching to the backstop must be at least twenty-five feet in width.

The 225 feet or 74.25 meter marking applies to male and female fast-pitch. Women's slow-pitch must be played in at least 250 feet, or 82.5 meters, of open area. Finally, the male slow-pitch leagues must observe a minimum marking of 275 feet or 90.75 meters.

An added note in the rules concerning field layout provides for a circle chalked from the pitcher's rubber. The sixteen-foot, or 5.28 meter, circle is drawn from that plate, eight feet, or 2.64 meters, in radius (see accompanying illustration). Any deviation

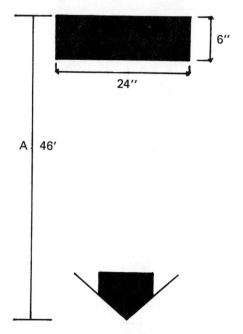

Official distances between the pitcher's rubber and home plate.

from the official field layout must be agreed upon in advance by the opposing leagues or teams. This particular rule allows softball to be played when the field does not, for one reason or another, meet all the standard measurements.

Pitching distances were also established many years ago. For men's fast-pitch, the length from the rubber to home plate is forty-six feet, or 15.18 meters. Female fast-pitch teams throw from a distance of forty feet, or 13.2 meters, while the slow-pitch leagues toss from forty-six feet, or 15.18 meters, in both men's and women's competition.

Some other important field measurements are the sixty feet, or 19.8 meter, markings between home and first base, from first to second, and so on. Also, the batter's box, which under the rules must be a three-foot, or 0.99 meter, by seven-foot, or 2.31 meter, enclosure. Listed along with the previously mentioned distances are the precise sizes of the catcher's box, coach's box and on-deck circle.

If one were to begin designing a softball field in the neighborhood park or schoolyard, it would be almost essential to invest first in a copy of the official rules and field dimensions such as one finds in this book. It will in the long run be the best preliminary move made. And since rules are changed from time to time, it is a smart idea to obtain the most recent edition of the rules. In that way one can keep abreast of any or all changes affecting the field layout.

We will now briefly go over the rules that govern the game of softball.

Rule One includes softball definitions. Examples of definitions are phrases such as appeal play, batted ball, dead ball, force out, illegal bat and so on. Over fifty-five definitions are included in Rule One.

Rule Two deals with the official dimensions of a softball field, and Rule Three explains in detail what may or may not be used in terms of equipment. Rule Four is concerned with the players and substitutions in softball. Section One of Rule Four says in effect that a team shall consist of nine fast-pitch players or ten slow-pitch players, depending on the game.

Section three of Rule Four covers a new addition to softball, the designated hitter rule. The other sections of Rule Four spell out the other criteria that must be met before a team may play a game or substitute after the game has begun.

Rule Five includes eight sections. Section One states that the choice of the first or last at-bat in the inning shall be decided by a toss of a coin unless otherwise noted in the rules of the league under which the schedule of games is being played. This last part of the rule is an out, so to speak, for the many leagues throughout the United States which must play under time and

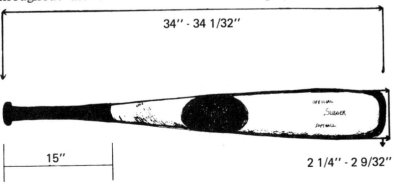

Official measurements for a softball bat.

inning limits. These limits allow more games to be played in a specific time span and therefore permit an increased number of people to participate.

Section Two of Rule Five gives the umpires full authority to decide whether a field is in suitable condition for play. Section Three puts in capsule form the definition of a regulation game. Sections Four through Eight discuss the scoring aspects of softball and what actually constitutes a run for one side or the other.

Rule Six has always been a controversial portion of the standards because it deals with pitchers. Due to the quickness of many pitchers, players often complain that they are bending or breaking the rules. The complaining occurs especially in the lower leagues, where many an umpire and player alike have trouble distinguishing a legal pitch from the illegal variety.

In any case, Section One is probably the area causing the most confusion, not because it isn't clear, but because many pitchers don't follow it to the letter. In essence, it states that a pitcher must have both feet firmly on the ground and in contact with the rubber before delivering a pitch. The pitcher must also come to a complete stop facing the batter, with the ball held in both hands in front of the body. The position described must be maintained for at least one second, but the ball thrown before ten seconds have elapsed since the previous pitch.

The reason this particular rule causes problems is that many pitchers try to get the edge by working more quickly and positioning themselves a touch closer to the plate. Many pitchers also violate a part of Section Two which covers the actual pitch. To be a legal pitch in accordance with the rules, one must have the pivot foot in contact with the pitching rubber until the other foot touches the ground.

Quite often a pitcher will come off the rubber with considerable force, completely forgetting about keeping contact as stated in the rules. I use the word forgetting loosely, because most good pitchers will utilize this technique to get an edge. Sections Three through Eleven in Rule Six cover completely the other facets of pitching, such as when a "no pitch" is to be called by an umpire or what really constitutes a legal pitch.

Rule Seven is the longest of the statutes, with thirteen sections;

it covers batting. Among the items discussed in Sections One through Thirteen are the definitions of a strike, ball, fair ball, foul ball and foul tip. Included in detail is when a batter will be judged out and when he may remain at bat. Rule Seven should be read by everyone who plays softball. The contents could actually win a game under certain circumstances.

Section Eight of Rule Eight makes important reading for anyone who plays, because it deals with base running. As a base runner, there are several ways to be called out besides being tagged by a fielder with the ball or in a force situation. Most are common knowledge but are sometimes forgotten in the heat of a game.

Rule Nine has two detailed sections. One section interprets when a ball is considered dead and the other covers when the ball is legally in play.

Rule Ten concerns itself with umpires. The powers and duties of an umpire are written in concise fashion so that everyone may understand what their function is. This section of the rules, if read by a player, coach or fan will give one a better idea of what to look for in an umpire's performance on the field.

Rules Eleven and Twelve detail protests and scoring. Rule Eleven has seven sections on protests: when a protest may be lodged, how one goes about protesting a game, and several other items about a protest are there for anyone to see.

Rule Twelve has eight sections on scoring. These sections talk about the box score, runs batted in and many of the subtle aspects of scoring a softball game. Both of these rules are very important. Certain sections in Eleven and Twelve can in the final analysis also win a softball game.

Plainly and simply, few people besides umpires are students of the rulebook. Many, in fact, are quite ignorant when it comes to the field layout and rules that govern the game. Most just come out to play and hope the calls "don't go against them."

One way to insure that you are getting a fair call is to know the rules. For at that point, you will either argue vehemently, or keep quiet. Sooner or later the umpires will take notice of that fact and remember it in future ball games.

4

Softball Overview

The game of softball, as we have discussed, is an easy sport to learn. It is, in its simplest form, a pastime that requires little technical knowledge to play.

However, that premise is not true when highly talented athletes competing in league or tournament play are involved. For these men, women, boys and girls, the sport of softball is played in a sophisticated fashion that utilizes strategy, tenacity, and plain hard work.

It involves many hours of concentrated practice to become world-class. Numerous teams are of that caliber and most all would concur that the glamour, so to speak, is during the game or at the awards ceremony.

Most can tell stories of the laborious practices and offseason activities that one engages in to keep in shape for the long campaign.

There is no doubt that a person must be a very dedicated soul to excel in the higher reaches of softball. He or she must also possess a love for the game that is almost unmatched in sport. Because of its amateur status, it provides very little monetary gain. Therefore, almost all of the players involved today make tremendous sacrifices in order to become great in softball.

A team wishing to follow this road must be very organized. They must properly select sponsors, managers, coaches, and players. After this is accomplished, some of the items contained in this chapter will become very important.

After a team has been assembled, it is essential that everyone feels he is helping the unit win in some way. Unfortunately, most clubs have a great deal of difficulty molding together a group of talented athletes. Generally speaking, most teams have players from all walks of life. This is a prevalent situation with obvious flaws. Ideally, a team would be clones of one another and all the members would know what the others were thinking.

Many teams attempt to solve this problem by holding frequent club meetings. This gives the players time to vent their frustrations and relieve tensions brought on by the pressure atmosphere that sometimes exists in softball, as with any sport. Most managers and coaches agree team meetings are a helpful tool at any level of play.

Besides meetings, another way everyone can feel involved in a team's success is if all the squad members have explicit duties. Numerous teams in leagues around the country allow players to sit on the bench with nothing to do. Consequently, some will stew about not playing. This can be avoided by assigning non-playing jobs that clearly benefit the team.

Some of the things players can do from the bench include trying to steal signals, keeping performance charts, scorebooks, and warming up players preparing to go into the game. Also shouting to the catcher on steals and squeeze plays can contribute directly to victory. One need only use the imagination to come up with helpful things players on the bench can do to help win a game. A team with a good record over a long season has players alert and into the game down to the last man.

In addition to doing these basic dugout jobs, it would be wise to develop a good memory as to what a batter likes to hit and what a pitcher likes to throw in a key situation. The result of all this work may be just two or three games won by the bench in the course of a season, but one of those wins could conceivably bring a tourney or league championship. If nothing else, it will help build morale, both on the bench and in the field, where the players will certainly notice and gain from the bench activity.

Naturally, teams excelling in softball have more than just

bench strength. They must also possess better than adequate hitting, fielding and pitching.

What we have discussed up to this point is basically what everyone can do to win games and still remain happy. What has and will be discussed can be used in some degree by every level of competition.

BATTING ORDER

The batting order in softball is very important. Equally crucial is the execution of basic softball skills by the players in that lineup. Such techniques as the bunt and sacrifice fly are good examples.

Keeping the skills of your players in mind, for that is the ultimate determinant of your batting order, an ideal leadoff person is one who frequently gets on base. He or she should hit for a solid average, be a good base runner, have a good eye at the plate, and excel at the art of bunting.

The number two person in the order should have many of the same capabilities as the leadoff hitter; being a good batter is a must because this person will frequently be required to move a base runner along. In many cases he or she will have to hit behind the runner, or at least to the right side. A good second batter is invaluable in a lineup.

The third batter will in many situations be the best all-around player on the squad. He or she is one who hits for power and average, and can run the bases with authority.

In the clean-up or fourth position, a team will want a player known to hit and drive in runs under clutch circumstances. He or she must also be an offensive threat in the same manner as the number three hitter, and also carry a healthy average. If a team should have two players who fit the three and four hitter mold, it would be a smart move to have the faster runner hitting in the third spot. This avoids the possibility of a slow third hitter holding up the fourth hitter in an extra base hit situation.

For the number five position, a manager will many times select a player who has good power but may not be hitting for a high average. In any case, the number five hitter will generally come to the plate many times with people on base. It is therefore hoped he will be able to drive in the runs.

The number six batter in the lineup is a player who possesses many of the same qualities as the first or second person in the order. If he or she can hit for power and run the bases well, it can be considered a bonus. Players seven and eight in the order fall into the same category as the sixth batter. They may be fairly weak hitters, but outstanding in the field. If they can hit with reasonable success it will prove to be a boon over the course of a season. Keep in mind also that the players at the bottom of the order many times start a rally which is carried through the top half and into the power spots. For some teams this can be a source of justifiable pride.

In most lineups a pitcher will bat ninth. There are several reasons for this. One, he or she is concentrating on pitching and finds little time to work on batting. Two, a pitcher will be placed ninth so that he or she can rest more often in the course of a game. However, it is to be noted that some of the great pitchers are also tremendous hitters. For that reason, it may be smart to bat a pitcher higher in the order.

In discussing the ideal people for certain spots in the order, we are, of course, talking in generalities. Many managers simply don't have the personnel to create the ideal lineup and must work with the talent available.

In later chapters we will discuss hitting, fielding, catching and pitching in greater detail. Also included will be some of the team strategies involved in playing softball. In an overall sense, however, the game of softball is won with excellent pitching, an iron defense and a solid hitting attack.

In fast-pitch softball games, the scores are in most cases on the low side. This is a common occurrence because the pitching often dominates the other team's offense. For this reason, the offensive team must execute properly and do the small things that add up. One important tool which must be mastered in softball is the bunt for a base hit. Also, possessing the ability to move the runner who has reached first base along with a sacrifice bunt is a key ingredient over the course of a season. In practically all situations with a runner on first and no outs, the team at bat will bunt. But many times everyone in the park is expecting the bunt play to move the man along, and if the bunt is not executed properly, it can result in a double play, wiping out a potential rally.

With runners on first and second and less than two out, a bunt is again an important tool. A well-bunted ball avoids the possibility of a double play and in many cases moves the runners along into scoring position. At that point a team could score with a sacrifice fly or by a ball hit on the ground to the right side.

Most managers will agree that over the course of a game and season that it is a smart practice to hit away, or attempt a steal of second, where a team is expecting the standard play such as a sacrifice bunt. Sometimes using other strategies won't work, but it does keep the defense guessing. It is not always a good idea to exercise only one option in a given situation. There must be times, especially when a team is slumping, that a coach goes for the big play.

In addition to what has been mentioned, there are several other strategies, such as the sacrifice and the squeeze play, as well as the various stealing plays, the run-and-hit and hit-and-run among them. Most agree a good number should be tried at different times during the season to see which ones will work for your team.

Before we close this chapter, it should be said that softball is meant to be fun above all. For that reason, it would be an intelligent move to always reevaluate a team's potential and ability, before tackling a caliber of ball that is too advanced. Basically, stick to the level of competition best suited for your team. In the long run it will save time and money, and the season will be enjoyed more by everyone concerned.

5

Conditioning

To play any sport, one must be in good condition. For a softball player physical conditioning may be the difference between winning and losing.

Good examples of situations when a softball player must be in good condition are in an extra-inning game or when a team is going through the loser's bracket in a tournament, in which a club may be forced to play five games in a row in the dead of summer.

For a pitcher it could be many innings of action in one day or for an outfielder, several long sprints after balls that end up going into foul territory.

If the players are not in shape physically, any of the aforementioned situations, and many more, could be their eventual undoing. It is paramount that players in softball keep in reasonably good condition.

Being properly conditioned will save one from a lot of the pulled muscles, sore legs and other problems associated with being overweight or out of shape entirely.

To reach the peak of condition, players use many methods. They utilize different exercises and participate in varied off-season activities to stay in form.

In fact, it is safe to say that no two players are alike in their physical and mental approach to softball. This is true from someone playing recreation ball to a softball veteran. For that reason alone it would be difficult to lay out an exact plan for a player

(Left) Ray Allena running in the outfield. It is very important that a player run to loosen his or her muscles before a game. (Right) Jim is stretching his back muscles by doing a roll-over and holding it in place for a few seconds at a time.

to follow for getting in shape before the season opens, or to guide him or her in their mental approach to softball.

So in this chapter we will discuss conditioning with some of the players involved in the book. Also, we will cover basic stretching and conditioning exercises for the different positions and conclude with a look at the treatment of minor sports injuries not requiring a doctor's care.

In the final analysis however, one will have to sit down and round out a program best suited for his own approach to the game.

In this chapter we will concentrate primarily on three areas: off-season conditioning, in-season conditioning, and the pre-game warmup period.

OFF-SEASON CONDITIONING

During the months when softball is not being played a player should ideally maintain a level of athletic involvement approaching that of his or her season's output. This can be accomplished by the setting up of rigorous off-season sporting activities that require the use of reflexes and strength. Pitcher Ty Stofflet says, "I run in the off-season whenever possible. I definitely play a lot of ping-pong. It is one of the best games I've found for keeping my coordination and remaining sharp in the off-season. I also bowl, because it's my opinion that a softball pitcher must keep his or her arm active all year around. For that reason, I start throwing a few weeks before the season starts. The only other thing I do consistently is use hand grips to strengthen my wrists. I try and use the grips three or four times a week while I'm relaxing or taking in a television show."

K. G. Fincher says, "I tend to gain some weight in the off-season, so I diet around January to drop off some of the excess weight. I play racquetball which helps my quickness. Also, I do a little running to build up my legs. Basically, anything that is good for your reflexes and strength will work in the off-season."

"In the off-season," Jim Marsh comments, "I play basketball and will run a little bit. I also keep active by playing racquetball Any exercise that is good for hand-eye coordination I'll do at one time or another. I feel wrist strength is important so I do exercises to work on them."

Mike Parnow remarks, "I run all the time. I never stop running even during the season. I run abut three miles a day, three times a week. Plus I play basketball in several leagues. The basketball keeps me quick and agile. An important factor in softball is keeping the extra weight off the body. I try and hold my off-season weight around what I intend to carry in the season."

"I've played flag football in the past and I bowl at least twice a week," observes Ray Allena. "I also play some racquetball and watch my weight closely to keep in shape."

In addition to the activities mentioned by the players are sports such as handball, squash or even badminton. Any sport that will exercise the entire body and contribute to keeping the competitive edge is good for an athlete in the off-season.

A person, besides engaging in various sports activities, will want to do specific exercises like the toe-touchers, sit-ups, jumping jacks, push-ups and shoulder rolls. These are fairly simple and should require only a little time each day. Since off-season conditioning is so important, a player may want to write out an exercise schedule to follow each day, including whatever activities he or she may be doing to keep in shape.

IN-SEASON CONDITIONING

After the season begins one is primarily concerned with maintaining top form and avoiding those injuries caused by not keeping in good shape. This also requires eating correctly in the days prior to a game and keeping reasonably active to sustain a competitive edge.

Tournament teams play most of their games on the weekends with a few games during the week over the course of a season. It is therefore important to engage in exercises that will keep one in condition between games.

Mike Parnow mentioned his running even during the season. Ty Stofflet says, "I run twenty to twenty-five miles a week up until June 1st. Then I stop and do other exercises because I feel by that time I have my legs built to full capacity. Legs are a big factor. If your legs are weak and your arm strong, you'll be fighting a losing battle. Staying in shape during the season is a significant factor in winning games."

Ray Allena feels staying in shape is critical because, "the aches and pains at the end of a season will really start to tire you. If a player can avoid problems by staying in good condition, it will help one be strong at the tail end of a season."

Continuing to do the various exercises, plus keeping a good diet, will help maintain a level of consistency for both the once-a-week player or the guy or girl who is playing tournament ball each weekend for over six months.

PRE-GAME CONDITIONING

Before a player steps onto any sort of playing field for a game, he or she should go through a period of stretching and loosening-up exercises that prepare the body for the rigors ahead. In the case of a softball player, one must consider the stop-and-go nature of the game.

Because a player must sprint after a ball or make a quick throw only a few times a game, we can plainly see the importance of a good pre-game warm-up program. Unfortunately, very few of us have the capacity to pick up a ball, for example, and throw it as hard as we can, or take off on a dead sprint, without injuring ourselves if we haven't warmed up properly.

So before a game, players can be found doing many exercises. Ideally, all should involve some running, stretching, and throwing. Also the proper use of uniform undershirts on cool or cold days to retain heat helps considerably, as does the use of jackets by the pitchers after warming up. Ty Stofflet recommends a pitcher wear a jacket after warming up, no matter what the temperature in the park.

K. G. Fincher's pre-game ritual is probably similar to many players. He says, "I try and stay away from eating much on the day of a game. Also, I'll spend time thinking about the game as much as possible. I feel the mental approach is very important. In pre-game warm-up I use a weighted softball for psychological reasons. I'm not sure it helps physically, but mentally one feels stronger."

"Some pitchers will simulate game conditions when throwing in their warm-up. They stand with both feet on an imaginary rubber

Mike is demonstrating a very popular exercise. It involves assuming the position shown and moving the head toward the toe very slowly so as not to pull any muscle.

This is another very popular exercise among players. In this photo, Mike is stretching his leg muscles. It is a good idea to do several exercises before a practice or game to loosen up.

and so on. For myself, I prefer to warm up by walking into the pitch. I don't throw the ball hard in warm-up, and generally stand about sixty feet from the person I'm playing catch with. The individual, however, must experiment and find what pre-game procedures are best for him or her, be they pitchers, catchers, infielders or outfielders."

Mike Parnow says, "If possible I try to eat a good breakfast. I would rather eat a good breakfast and play all day than eat between games. I don't like to play with a meal in my stomach; it feels like it weighs me down. I may eat a candy bar for quick energy."

"Before a game I'll stretch. I run out to the fence and back several times. From there I'll work on my back and touching my toes. Then I'll do eight to ten sit-ups and begin sprinting. Finally, I'll start throwing, soft at first and then speeding it up as my arm gets loose."

Whatever your off-season, in-season or pre-game ritual is, be sure it covers your specific needs adequately. If you have a history of hamstring pulls for instance, it would of course be advisable to spend more time warming up those muscles. That goes for all sore muscles, bad backs and the like.

In the off-season develop a stringent program for exercise. It could actually prolong your career considerably. Then during the season maintain a consistent schedule on game days and off days. This too may help a lot further down the line.

INJURIES

Most injuries people suffer should be checked by a doctor to make sure they are not of a serious nature. Many, however, will fit into the minor category and can be treated adequately by the individual.

Blisters on the fingers and feet give players fits, especially the pitcher. Finger blisters can be avoided by keeping the fingernails short and covering the area daily with Benzoin, commonly called tuf-skin. If a blister should form, it can be drained with a sterilized needle. At that point, it whould be left open to heal and sprayed again with Benzoin.

One will want to clean out an open foot blister completely and then use a compress. If it is not open, it should be covered by a bandage.

For sliding burns, it is good to shave the area around the wound and clean it well. Then apply a disinfectant to the wound and put a gauze pad over it. Change the pad daily to keep it clean.

A sore arm is relieved, of course, by not throwing. But to help it along one may apply a heat pack to it or take a hot shower holding the affected muscles under direct spray.

There are many other small injuries that can add up over the course of a season. Minor sprains, charlie horses, and pulled muscles are good examples. All can be treated by the player as long as they are not serious. If any of the conditions persist, it would be a wise move to consult a doctor immediately. An unchecked injury can cost a player several games or an entire season if found to be worse than first thought.

6

Pitching

Like many team sports, softball has its key position. And as with the other sports, this one position very often controls the flow of a game.

In fast-pitch softball, the most important spot on the field is in the center of the diamond. That is where the pitcher works. A good softball pitcher will help a team to a very large degree over the course of a season.

To attain greatness in softball as a pitcher takes years of practice and unwavering dedication. The process is generally a slow one and therefore discourages many players from making the effort. The two fine contributors to this chapter on pitching, Ty Stofflet and K. G. Fincher, each spent many years learning the fundamentals of pitching before finally becoming champions of their sport.

A highly skilled pitcher is a joy to watch. Armed with a variety of pitches that can rise and drop at incredible speeds, he or she is capable of doing amazing things over the course of a game or season. Both Stofflet and Fincher, for example, know the feeling of throwing a perfect game with many strikeouts, or pitching in a tie ballgame that has stretched well beyond the normal seven innings. Before a pitcher can be expected to respond in situations like those described, he or she must have settled on a basic pitching motion and acquired a variety of pitches. After attaining these, a pitcher then must attempt to pitch wherever and whenever possible.

Most softball pitchers will agree that experience is the only way to become competent enough to lead a team to victory consistently.

The majority of softball pitchers in fast-pitch competition use what is known as the windmill delivery, as opposed to the slingshot or figure-eight style. A more detailed look at softball deliveries begins with the windmill.

WINDMILL

The windmill delivery starts with both hands held together at the waist. Then one of two techniques is used. The first one has a pitcher bringing his or her hand forward, then high over the head and all the way around, forming a large circle just before the ball is released.

With the other, a pitcher will bring the glove and ball hands to his or her chest, face, or above the head. Then the arms come down again and the pitcher removes the ball hand from the glove and uses the full circle motion before letting the ball leave the hand.

FIGURE-EIGHT

The figure-eight is a seldom used delivery and one that requires a good deal of practice to master. Basically, it involves moving the arm in a figure-eight motion as you bring the ball to the front of your body before the release. At the beginning of the forward movement the arm should move well away from the body to start the eight and end with it close to the hip and leg.

The figure-eight was first used to increase velocity, but because of the difficulty in controlling the subsequent throw, it has become less and less popular as the years go by. Many of the early pitchers in softball history utilized the figure-eight style with ample success.

SLINGSHOT

The slingshot delivery is one that has become very common in recent seasons. It is used in both the lower and higher classifications of softball, and it seems equally popular among men and women.

The pitch is thrown by bringing the arm straight back and up, until the hand is over the head, and then reversing that path and pulling the arm through the motion at a high rate of speed. Because

This is the windmill pitching sequence, taken with the ball at the top of K. G. Fincher's head and concluding with the release of the pitch. Note: The grip in the second photo shows Fincher throwing a rise-ball.

the arm assumes only a partial circle, it is not called a windmill delivery. Due to the short thrusting motion of a slingshot pitch, it has become especially prevalent among beginning pitchers who normally suffer control problems at the start.

K. G. demonstrating a popular delivery called the slingshot. The ball comes to the top of the head, then is reversed through the motion and released.

TIPS FOR BEGINNERS

Besides the basic deliveries, many things go into the art of pitching. At the beginning, Ty Stofflet advises, "Try to keep your arm as close to your body as possible when throwing. After you finish your stride upon completion of the pitch, your foot should end up in a direct line with the catcher."

"If you're right-handed, it should be the left foot that ends in the line; and if you're a lefty, the right foot should end in front. If the foot is off to the side, a pitch may not have the accuracy it needs.

K. G. just after releasing a pitch.

"Another problem beginners suffer is that they are continually off balance when they stride. This is corrected by constant practice and proper throwing techniques.

"Perhaps the most important aspect of pitching is control. You must have control before ever thinking about putting something on the ball. I know from experience that walking batters will get you into trouble. After gaining control, work and master one pitch at a time.

"Finally, avoid using too much arm in the pitch and develop a quick snap of the wrist as you bring the ball through. When you can combine this with a body thrust off the rubber, you'll be surprised at the increase of speed."

K. G. Fincher also relies on a good snap of the wrist for speed and says, "Timing and rhythm are also very important. Then

This photo shows the positioning of the feet just before the release of a pitch.

comes the good release based on putting all the various factors together. After a few years, one will be better able to make adjustments which will improve a pitcher's performance."

A good thought for the beginner and veteran pitcher to keep in mind is something Ty Stofflet says: "Many times a pitcher has the tendency to work too fast. One must always think before letting a pitch go. Concentration is also a big factor. Sometimes a pitcher can get lazy and that's where the trouble begins."

DIFFERENT PITCHES

In order to be successful a pitcher must develop pitches that "move" on the way to the plate. Most pitchers will try to develop a rise, drop, change-up, curve, and variations on all four in their repertoire of pitches.

The development of pitches is important because it is a well known fact that players will not be fooled by straight pitches even if they are thrown extremely fast.

K. G. Fincher says, "The game has changed, no doubt about it. In the last five years alone there is a big difference. The players seem to be better hitters. A pitcher used to dominate the other team 100 percent in some cases. Now they can't.

"You have to use all the pitches to be successful in softball today. I can remember in the Sixties if one didn't get fifteen strikeouts, he considered it a bad night. Now if you get ten strikeouts you've done well.

"Another factor in using all the pitches in softball today revolves around the lineups. It used to be the first three or four guys in a lineup were tough outs, so against them you threw hard and then slacked off a little with the others. Now you have to bear down and mix the pitches against the entire lineup."

RISE-BALL

The rise-ball is one of the pitcher's best friends. A lively, well-thrown rise may "jump" as it hurtles towards the plate, while at the same time moving upwards.

The basic rise is thrown several ways, but the most common method is the one K. G. Fincher uses. About throwing the rise

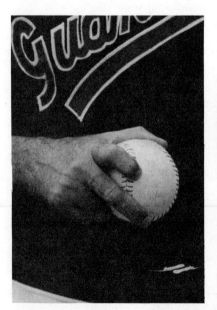

(Left) This is the grip for the rise ball as shown by K. G. Fincher. (Right) K. G. showing good eye contact with the target on his way to releasing a rise ball.

he says, "I tuck the index finger up on the seams and kick it out of my hand. The ideal way to get it rising is to have a four seam rotation on the way to the plate.

"Using all four seams increases the friction of the ball against the air. That friction makes it move. If the softball was like a billiard ball, you couldn't do anything with it. In throwing the pitch you have to make sure it's rotating."

Ty Stofflet comments, "I throw mine like a forkball overhand. I use my three fingers in the middle and separate them as far as I can. At the release point, I push the ball between these fingers. I keep my arm and wrist close to my body and snap upwards on the throw. Most pitchers will try different grips until they find one that feels good for them. I use three rise-balls: a straight-rise, a rise-up and a rise-curve."

DROP-BALL

Of all pitches, the drop may be the easiest to master and yet become the toughest pitch to hit in a given repertoire. Based on the release of the ball and with the help of gravity, a drop-ball will sink on the way to the plate.

One of the several grips that can be used to throw a drop ball. Note: Finger across the seams to help get proper rotation for the pitch.

The drop-ball is a pitch batters will be fooled by, but like the others does require a fair amount of time to throw with success.

K. G. Fincher is a master of the drop and says, "I use two fingers straight off to roll the ball and get a down rotation. Just like the rise, a ball must have rotation up or down to be effective. Pitchers sometimes roll their drops over so far that it tends to go down and move in. That particular pitch has been a good one for me."

Ty Stofflet says about the drop-ball, "I release mine almost like one would release a bowling ball: two fingers across the seams, and I end up using a follow-through, again like when bowling. With that basic pitch, I have developed three off-speed drops to help confuse the batter."

CURVE-BALL

A softball curve is held and thrown almost like a rise-ball. The idea is to get the ball to break across the batter's body. There is a strategy involved in throwing a curve.

A pitcher may aim the ball at the batter so that it will break

This grip may be used for a curve or rise-curve.

over the inside corner, or throw it at the center of the plate and let it break outside.

Most top-notch pitchers refrain from using the curve because the movement of the ball is neither up nor down but on the same plane, which gives the batter a better chance of hitting the ball. A poorly thrown curve can very easily end up in the cheap seats.

Some pitchers will use a combination pitch called a rise-curve which is thrown by putting the middle and index fingers on the "side" of the ball and snapping the wrist on release. This release will cause the ball to rise and break on the way to the plate.

CHANGE-UP

The change of pace or change-up is a pitch everyone should have. Used properly in key situations, it can be another pitch that wipes away a potential rally. Some pitchers will never possess a good change of pace pitch primarily because they do not think it is necessary. However, it stands to reason—the more pitches, the better one will be.

This is one of the proper grips for a fast-pitch change-up.

K. G. shows the release of a change-up and the palm exposed as the arm comes up in a dramatic fashion.

K. G. Fincher, on throwing his change-up, says, "I'm palming the ball and letting it roll out of my hand. I throw a straight change."

Other pitchers use many off-speed pitches which can be considered change-ups. Occasionally, a pitcher will exhibit a knuckle-ball which is thrown (preferably against a wind) with little or no rotation on the ball. The knuckler literally tosses around in the air currents and is extremely hard to control. Even a master pitcher like Stofflet uses a knuckle-ball only once in a great while. Says he, "I really don't know where it will end up, so I can't afford to throw it very much."

After a pitcher settles on one delivery and learns how to use pitches effectively, he or she must be aware of the other facets of pitching that produce a winner.

PITCHING STRATEGY

"One thing I remember is what a batter did the previous time up," says Ty Stofflet. "What a batter does and does not like to hit should be noted by the pitcher. The time you forget a good rise-ball hitter is the time you'll get hurt." However, Stofflet hastens to note, "That doesn't mean you won't throw your best pitch to a batter because they hit it. In some situations you will have to throw your best pitch and wait for the results."

A smart pitcher will seldom throw "fat" strikes, meaning those down the center of the plate, and will purposely pace himself or herself through a game. Pitchers never know if they will be called on to go extra innings on a particular day. If they are, he or she must be ready with the energy required to go the distance. After the physical preparation comes the mental approach to pitching.

K. G. Fincher says, "When I walk out to the rubber, I feel I will not lose. I have the attitude that nobody can beat me. If I didn't follow this thinking, I wouldn't have the kind of confidence a pitcher needs to win consistently in this game."

THE FIELDING PITCHER

After the ball is thrown, a pitcher becomes an infielder. He or she can aid the club considerably by keeping as many balls as possible from going up the middle, and by backing up the proper bases on hits to the outfield.

If he or she does that and combines it with the proper mental and physical approach to the game, they will be better softball players. Good pitchers agree it takes years to put it all together, but when one does, look out!

CATCHER

The one position that many times goes without notice or recognition in softball is the catcher's spot.

Yet it is one of the most important positions on the field. A catcher is a member of a special breed. He or she must endure many bumps and bruises during a season.

The catching position requires a quick thinker and a person with an accurate arm. And since catchers in most cases call the pitches, they must also become students of the game, learning the strengths and weaknesses of opposition hitters and remembering them for future games.

Jim Marsh shows a good target to the pitcher
by extending his glove towards the pitcher.

IN THE BEGINNING

It can be difficult for a softball player to make the adjustment
to catching a softball pitcher. But for the former baseball catcher
it can be tougher still. For one thing, the ball is assuming a different rotation than baseball. This can be confusing for a new catcher
trying to make an adjustment between the two sports.

Sound advice comes from Jim Marsh when he says, "It's a good
tip for someone starting out to just plain watch the ball. Don't
watch anything but the ball all the way to the glove. You want
to pick it up as it comes off the hip of the pitcher. A catcher should
also avoid watching the whole windup."

"The only thing he or she should be concentrating on is the
release and the ball on the way to the glove."

CATCHER AND PITCHER COMMUNICATION

"As a catcher," says Jim Marsh, "I never have a set plan for a
game. I always want to use the variety of pitches available. As the
game begins, I watch closely to see what pitches are moving and
working. If the pitcher is going smoothly, I'll make a mental note

(Left) Jim breaks from his crouch position and comes up ready to throw the ball. (Right) Many times a catcher will have to block the ball from going through to the backstop. Jim shows proper form in blocking the wild pitch.

to watch very intently around the middle innings to make sure he is not just going through the motions. A pitcher must always concentrate on every pitch."

"In the late innings I look to the pitcher to tell me the truth as to whether he's tired. Also I keep a sharp eye out because some have such pride they'll continue on and on even when they're tired."

As the innings progress a pitcher with a lead may tend to relax or, if behind in a game, start to give up. It is the nature of pitchers to go through various emotions during a game. When Marsh senses a change of mood he goes to work. "With some I'll act mad, some I have to pump up. Others just need a litle talking to for them to get back on the track. I've never caught two pitchers alike, never two that were even similar. For this reason a catcher and pitcher must have good communication to get the best performance out of both."

CATCHER'S STRATEGY

There are many situations a catcher must think about in the course of a game behind the plate. If the team you are playing

Jim has good arm extension as he releases
the throw towards second base.

is unfamiliar to you, the first time through their batting order will
show you the hitters. As each one comes to the plate, glance
to see if he or she looks and stands like a hitter and then swings
like one. Make a mental note for future reference. Also analyze
each situation carefully so that you make throws to correct bases
and are aware of any play likely to occur in a game.

Further, a catcher must always be on guard against a wild
pitch; when calling for the various pitches he or she must have the
glove ready to move where the ball may end up.

One must be aware at all times of any pickoff signals given
by teammates and hustle perpetually.

CATCHER'S RAPPORT WITH THE UMPIRE

"I never have trouble with umpires," says Jim Marsh. "The
game is so fast that it isn't a good idea to get upset over a call.
It could hurt your play. Generally, if an umpire misses a pitch,
you'll get one back later. Finally, don't *ever* try to show an
umpire up. Just develop a working relationship with the ump and
keep quiet about particular calls."

7

Fielding

Softball games are won with good pitching and ironclad defense. Because the game is played on a smaller field than baseball, it is imperative that the fielders possess quickness of mind and body, and a thorough understanding of his or her position.

One must be aware at all times. Infielders are tested often in softball as balls reach their gloves at a high rate of speed due to the relatively short distance between batter and fielder. They must react in the correct way. Anything less will produce a physical or mental error, and trouble for the team.

Outfielders are required to get a good jump on the ball, make the catch if they can and throw to the proper base or to the cut-off person depending on the circumstance. Both the infielder and outfielder can contribute by making the correct decision when it counts. All fielders must know before each pitch what the count on the batter is, how many outs there are and what they will do with the ball should it be hit in their direction.

Many players excel in this area and feel their defensive skills are what help them stand out in softball. These players often work all year round to improve their game. This aspect is sometimes forgotten as one watches a good defensive player make a great play. To become a high caliber defensive player takes countless hours of ground balls for the infielders and fly balls for the outfielders, followed closely by the knowledge acquired through experience in softball.

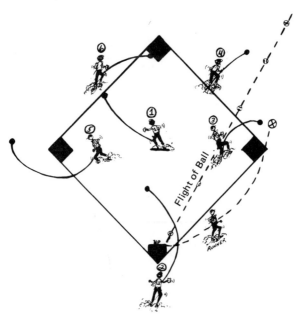

Infield movement with nobody on base and a single to right field.

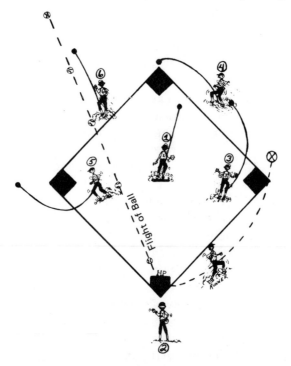

Infield movement with nobody on base and a single to left field.

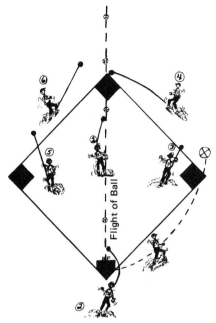

Infield movement with nobody on base and a single to center field.

Almost anyone can be a good defensive player provided he or she is willing to take the time to learn a particular position and then apply the pride and desire that separates the mediocre ballplayer from the very good one.

INFIELDERS

As briefly mentioned, the infielder in softball is very close to the batter which forces the ballplayer to react quickly. He or she must be alert and quick with the glove. These adjustments and others will become second nature with experience. However, there are some fundamentals which must be remembered no matter what position you are playing.

Mike Parnow, one of the best softball infielders in the nation, says, "One must keep the glove down and open at all times. Remember, you can always come up on a ball but almost never go down. Stay down, for if the ball takes a bad hop you will want to have it deflect off your chest and hopefully stay in front of the body so you can pick it up and throw the runner out."

"It is very important to know what the game situation is," continues Mike. "And also to know what your teammates are

(Left) Mike Parnow shows excellent reactions to a hit ball. Note that the glove is almost touching the ground. (Right) An infielder must be able to come in quickly on many ground balls

thinking on the field. For instance, if a man is on base, try to know and analyze what kind of runner he may be. Size him up. That goes for the hitter also. Does he or she look like a speedy runner, or a slow power hitter? Then communicate with the other fielders to make sure everyone knows what is happening. This will help in determining what to do if the ball comes in your direction. You have to be a thinker in softball."

Many beginning infielders in softball have an understandable fear of playing in on the batter, such as in a bunt situation. About this Parnow comments, "I don't think about it a whole lot, although there are times when it crosses my mind. If someone rams one down my throat, I'll be thinking about it the next time they come to bat. Overall I feel in my own mind that I'll catch anything close. This feeling is an important one for an infielder."

THIRD BASE

Playing third base in softball is a difficult task. Mike Parnow played at every infield position and now plys his trade at third base. He says about positioning at third, "I always play in towards

The following four-photo sequence shows Mike using the proper method of barehanding a ball and making a throw to first. This is one of the most difficult plays in softball.

home plate or tight at the corner as they say in softball. I do this unless the batter is likely to be hitting away with little chance of a bunt.

If a power hitter should bunt, then he or she is doing the defense a favor. In general, I play close to the line because in softball almost any hit down the line will result in a double at least. This positioning is especially valid in a low scoring game where one run could decide the game."

A third baseman will also want to remember that a ball hit with anything on it will give the defensive player a lot of time in which to throw a runner out. In many cases, the person at third will have more time to make a play than anyone else in the infield.

Also there can be no hesitation on a hit ball. Parnow says, "It's cut and dried, you make the play or you don't. If you hesitate, for example, by looking at second for an unlikely double play, then you may have lost the runner going to first. Hesitation in softball equals trouble. That goes for any position."

SHORTSTOP

The shortstop position is one that requires a quicker release than any other. Many times he or she will have to throw across the diamond in a minimum of time to get a runner out.

A softball shortstop will play his position somewhat deep if nobody is on base. This way a good deal of ground can be covered on both the glove hand side and bare hand side.

Actual positioning in a particular game will of course depend on the situation and hitter at the plate.

The position demands mobility because a player must be able to make a play and throw coming in, and chase a pop fly to the shallow portion of the outfield. Also a shortstop will at times be the only player who can reach a pop foul down the third base line.

Perhaps the toughest play in terms of agility is one in which a ball is hit into the hole between third and short; a player must backhand the ball and throw in one motion to get the runner out at first.

In addition, a shortstop has the responsibility of starting a double play if the ball is hit to him or her, or covering second if the ball is hit to the right side.

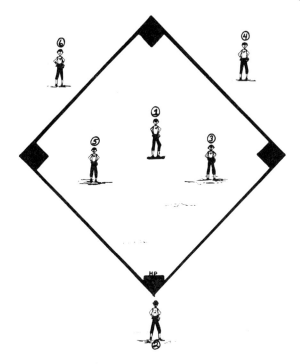

Infield depth in a bunt situation.

SECOND BASE

This spot requires having a person with very quick reactions and good softball sense. In a typical game the second baseman will be required to do many jobs. He or she must routinely field any ball hit in the second base area, cover first on a bunt attempt, cover second on a ball hit to the shortstop for the start of a double play, cover second on a steal attempt, or race back on a pop-up or foul ball to the right side.

To handle these chores and many more takes a player who can move to a spot after getting a good jump on the ball and one who analyzes a situation and reacts to it quickly and effectively.

FIRST BASE

A first baseman will be in on more plays than most any player on the field. Due to the nature of softball, there are several throws to first in every game. The athlete playing first should be extremely

(Top) "Zeke" McDowell, also a veteran of several national tournaments, and a player for the Guanella Brothers softball team, shows good form as he comes over to get in front of a ball at second base. (Bottom) Mike and Zeke team up in this photo to show the double play pivot at second base. A double play can instantly ruin a potential rally for the opposing team.

quick and very agile. He or she will have to play in close to the batter quite often to defend against the bunt.

A first baseman will also go to the bag at a dead run after a ball is hit to another infielder, then straddle the bag with the feet and wait for the throw. At the time a ball is released, the first baseman will make certain adjustments to catch the ball such as stretching for the throw or moving the feet to be in line with the ball.

In most cases, very little adjustment will be needed. However, there will be times when a throw is wide and a first baseman must leave the straddle position, catch the ball and tag the base before the runner gets there. He or she may also have to dig a ball out of the dirt, jump high or lean to the side to make an out.

Infield depth for a double play in fast-pitch.

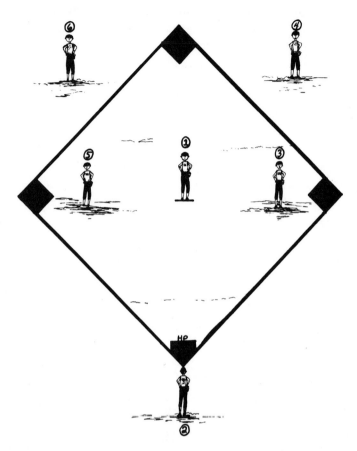

Regular infield depth in fast-pitch.

All in all, a first baseman must think on his or her feet, be slick with the glove, and play errorless ball a good deal of the time to be successful in softball.

OUTFIELDING

Ray Allena sums up the attitude of most outfielders when he says, "I take considerable pride in my outfielding. I love to chase down balls and throw guys out. In the outfield you get many crucial plays and a chance to act on them. One can make a game-saving catch or throw a person out going to second. It is a very exciting position to play."

(Top left) Ray Allena is in full control of his body as he races for a fly ball in the outfield. (Top right) Ray in full control going back in the proper manner on a fly ball. (Left) The sun may be in an outfielder's eyes at times. Here, Allena puts a hand up to block out the sun so that he can see the ball.

The outfielder in softball must know the game situation at all times. That includes knowing the count, how many outs there are and even the subtle factors such as how hard the wind is blowing and in what direction. The latter can greatly influence a long throw. He or she must also be sure-footed and able to throw quickly and on target to catch a runner taking an extra base.

In addition, the outfielder must get a good "jump" on the ball. Allena says, "See the ball hit the bat. Try to be moving when

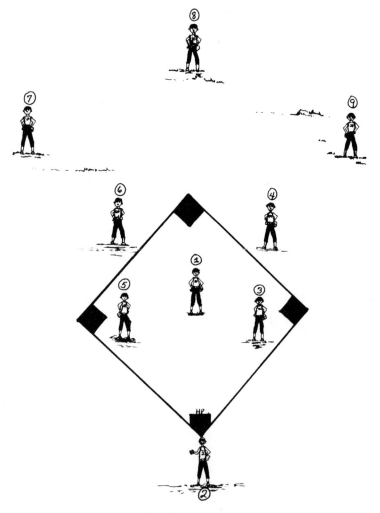

Outfield depth—deep.

Outfield depth—medium.

the ball is being pitched, mostly forward a couple of steps so that you're in motion by the time a ball is hit."

The outfielder should possess the ability to make almost any routine catch barring a freak shift of wind or some other factor that may change the course of the ball. Besides making the easy catch, an outfielder will want to have the capability of making the difficult plays also. As a final point, an outfielder can help the team by not trying to make the superhuman throw to a base or behind the runner. A good accurate throw to the cutoff man or to the base if necessary will do just fine. A valuable outfielder keeps his or her wits about himself or herself at all times and makes the proper throw after making the proper play on the ball.

It is a good idea for an outfielder to run to his or her position before a game and look at the general condition of the field as well as the distances to the fences and foul lines. If it is a night game, make sure you take several fly balls to check the lighting. Checking the grounds and lighting will help both on ground balls and fly balls to the outfield.

LEFT FIELD

The left fielder will see quite a bit of action every game. He or she must assume the ball will come in their direction with almost every batter. A left fielder will in most cases have the shortest throw of any outfielder. For that reason a club may want to use a weaker throwing outfielder in left, although that person must be very reliable on fly and ground balls. The left fielder will also back up the center fielder whenever necessary, and third base a good portion of the time to protect against overthrows. He or she must try to reach any foul ball down the left field line.

On ground balls to the outfield, a player should get down close to the ground and scoop the ball into the glove.

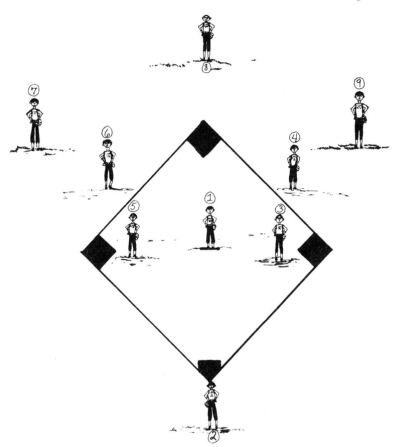

Outfield depth—shallow.

CENTER FIELD

A person occupying this position must have leadership qualities, good speed, sound judgment, and an accurate arm.

Many times the center fielder will position the other outfielders for a particular batter. He or she will also back up the other outfielders whenever possible.

About playing center, Ray Allena says, "I like to play the position shallow. My argument for this is that I see very few balls going over the heads of players, but too many balls are allowed to drop in over second base. There is a better chance of a person taking a check swing and dropping one than a player hitting the ball over your head, if you have decent speed."

"To hit it over your head, he or she has to know what they're doing and you won't see an outfielder misplaying that batter very often."

RIGHT FIELD

In right field, the player might need a stronger arm than the left fielder because the throws will be longer from that field.

A good strong throw from the outfield is seen in this photo as Ray unleashes one to the infield.

The right fielder must be prepared to back up the center fielder and all throws to first base, again for protection against the overthrow. A hustling right fielder can save many extra bases by getting to the throws that get past the first baseman.

The right fielder may also help a team by attempting to reach a foul ball lofted in the air on the right side of the diamond.

8

Batting

One of sports amazing stories is the consistent hitter in major fast-pitch softball. In men's action, consider a batter facing a pitcher forty-six feet away, throwing balls at over 100 miles per hour; not only are they coming fast, but moving in all directions.

To be able to hit good pitchers on a regular basis takes years of practice and hard work. This particular phase of the game finishes many players who have a good glove but simply cannot hit the pitching. Even in the lower levels of softball, players wash out for the same reason.

THE BEGINNING BATTER

Ray Allena is one of the game's best hitters. But at the start he too had trouble making contact with the ball. To improve, Allena comments, "I started studying pitchers. When I didn't have anything to do in the dugout I was watching different pitchers, to see if I could pick anything up."

"You would be surprised at how many pitchers tip off their rise and drop balls. I started "picking" pitches more often and it made me a better hitter. If you're at bat and you know what's coming, naturally it will help you. I also made it a point to remember every pitcher and what he was likely to throw at a certain time."

"As a rule never try to guess at a pitch. We have all done it at one time or another, but it's not to your advantage to try and guess because most times you won't be right. A guess hitter will find himself or herself swinging at too many bad pitches."

"Perhaps the only time you would 'guess hit,' so to speak, is in a situation where you feel the pitcher must come in with his best pitch."

"In my experience, I'd say half of the people who swing and miss, swing at pitches outside the strike zone. The key to hitting in softball is laying off the bad pitch. Anyone who is a fairly decent hitter will make contact with strikes."

Something Allena and many others did early in their careers was play a considerable amount of pepper with the pitcher. Allena suggests choking up on the bat and concentrating on putting the bat on the ball during the pepper game so the beginner can get used to the speed and rotation of the pitches.

STANCE AND STYLE

A batter's stance at the plate is very individual in nature. It is highly recommended that you try different stances in batting practice or under certain game conditions before settling on one

(Left) Ray Allena demonstrates a normal softball stance in this picture. (Right) Some players prefer what is shown here. It is a closed batting stance.

in particular. Keep in mind that very few batters share a common stance and swing at the plate.

"In the beginning," says Ray Allena, "I used a very open stance and almost faced the pitcher, just trying to hit the ball somewhere."

"As I started to make more and more contact, I brought my left foot in, (Allena bats righthanded) until I was finally back to the stance I brought from my pre-softball days in baseball."

"At times when I feel myself struggling at the plate, I will open up my stance and work on making better contact with the ball."

This stance is called open.

POWER HITTING

Most every hitter dreams of knocking a ball out of a park or clearing the bases with a triple. But in this sport, there are few power hitters, so these types of dreams remain quite elusive for the bulk of softball hitters.

Ray Allena says about power hitting, "In my opinion, you don't make yourself a power hitter. You are or you aren't. It depends on size and proper use of body weight. To be a power hitter you must put the entire body into the pitch.

Added to this factor is another called timing. Proper timing between body and swing as it goes into the pitch is a key."

Allena is known for his power hitting and yet confesses, "The only time I think longball is when it's a 'do or die' situation and we need a run or two very badly. In some cases, I will swing hard if the pitcher has no strikes on me. But I have found the harder a batter swings, the likelier the chance of pulling the head or making some other fundamental error which will cause a person to miss the ball or hit it poorly."

Good concentration and a powerful thrust towards the ball is captured in this photo of Ray Allena.

CONFIDENCE

Almost every batter has gone to the plate at one time or another just knowing they would hit the ball well. Unfortunately many batters will approach the plate in fear of a pitcher. When this happens the pitcher has the decided upper hand. About facing a pitcher, Allena says, "I take the attitude that nobody can get me out. So I go to the plate with confidence and take my swings. I have gone up against guys that were supposed to be tough that

I didn't think were. Then there were others with no reputation that gave me fits. A lot has to do with the kind of day the pitcher is having. In the end, though, it all comes down to his confidence against mine!"

BUNTING

The bunt is used frequently in softball, both as a way to move a runner into scoring position and as a method of reaching base safely.

These two uses of the bunt are respectively called the sacrifice bunt and the drag bunt. Both of these bunts do specific jobs and should be second nature to anyone playing the game of softball.

Mike Parnow lays down a sacrifice bunt. The sacrifice bunt technique shown here should be learned by all softball players.

SACRIFICE BUNT

The sacrifice bunt is used most often in softball to move a runner from first to second. It is also used frequently to advance runners from first and second into better scoring position at second and third.

To sacrifice bunt, one must stand in the batter's box and then turn at a forty-five degree angle towards the pitcher just as he or she is releasing the pitch. Once turned and facing the pitcher, a good bunter will bring the bat parallel to the ground, meanwhile sliding the top hand up the bat and holding it there with the fingertips. As the ball comes to the plate, the batter hopefully makes contact with the ball, sending it back towards the pitcher on the ground. Ideally, the runner on first will get to second with no problem. From there a team has several options and possibilities to pursue.

DRAG BUNT

The purpose of this bunt is to get a base hit. To be effective a high percentage of the time, the drag must come as a surprise to the other team. That means a hitter must look as if he or she will be swinging away when in fact the ball will be bunted. As the pitch is delivered, the batter will move his top hand up the bat as in the sacrifice bunt and begin to get a jump out of the box.

The drag bunt is one that may produce a base hit. Notice that Mike has started to move out of the box before the ball has reached the bat.

At the same time the ball hits the bat, the hitter has left the box on the way to first. The pressure is now on the defensive squad to throw the runner out.

Dropped at the proper time, a drag bunt can be a very good weapon. It is a strategy utilized in softball around the world.

Zeke McDowell is pictured here getting a good jump off the base after the ball leaves the pitcher's hand. Proper baserunning will help a team considerably over the course of a season.

BASERUNNING

Good baserunning over the course of a season will produce victories. To be a good baserunner takes proper technique, experience and a bit of speed for good measure.

The best baserunners in softball are those who cut the corners of the base sharply and thereby take the minimum number of steps to get around the bases.

In stealing, good baserunners get a quick jump when the ball leaves the pitcher's hand and then use the various slides available depending on the reaction of the defense.

There are different slides one can use when baserunning. Some players use a hook slide while others prefer a straight-in slide. In addition, one may see a pop-up slide which allows a runner to advance immediately if the ball gets away from the infielder. Also quite popular is the head first slide. This slide has the player diving towards the bag on the belly trying to get at least a hand on the base.

Softball experts agree that whatever style works for a player is

Zeke approaching third in preparation for a head first slide. Many players master several types of slides for use in games.

quite acceptable. Most players will try and become proficient with several sliding styles which is a very good idea.

The softball player that practices his or her baserunning and sliding techniques will before long see a marked improvement in overall playing ability. After all, it's great to get on base but what occurs after that is what really counts.

9

Softball as a Non-Profit Occupation

In looking at softball around the world, we can see a sport that is growing quite rapidly.

Because it is played, enjoyed, and supported primarily on a grass roots level, one can only assume that this trend will continue as it has right along.

In the United States, the future of softball appears very promising. Player and fan alike look to the day when the sport will receive national exposure on a regular basis.

Television programs such as the Tonight Show, Mike Douglas Show and many others have for years recognized the talent of softball players and had the big-time pitchers on, pitted against players from professional baseball teams. Inevitably, the softball pitcher easily outdueled the baseball player. Such stars as Willie Mays, Hank Aaron and Ted Williams have all tried to hit softball pitching with little or no success.

Softball games have had local coverage on radio and in newspapers for many seasons. But again it has been hit and miss in nature and certainly not on a regular basis. Such attention by the national media could catapult softball into a situation comparable with other sports.

Although the lack of network coverage has hindered the growth of softball, it certainly has not stopped its popularity with the millions of people currently playing this game. Nor has it cut down

on the tremendous growth seen each and every season now for
several years

With the sport now being considered for the Olympics and other
international competition, it will gain some of the recognition it
deserves. It can be said without argument that softball receives
the least media coverage of any of the sports in which such large
numbers of people participate.

Lack of publicity, in fact, has been the chief reason why professional softball has never made it in this country. This is substan-
tiated by the several groups who have tried and failed. The basic
idea is good but the poor planning and huge expenditures even-
tually force the leagues to fold.

In 1973, when K. G. Fincher signed with a newly formed
professional softball team operating out of Mobile, Alabama, he,
like the others involved, hoped that pro softball would make
it.

The league Fincher signed with had franchises in Toronto and
Montreal, Canada, Charlotte, North Carolina, St. Louis, a team
from Georgia, plus several teams located in Pennsylvania and
Fincher's club in Alabama.

Fincher recalls, "The idea of playing softball and being paid
well for it appealed to everyone. The short time I did play was
very enjoyable. It was first class all the way. When we came in
the locker room for a game, our uniforms were hung in the lockers
and the shoes were shined. But the travel costs and lack of
publicity got to be too much for the owners and the teams folded.
I can still remember the first game I pitched with the pro team. I
was throwing hard. I never have thrown a ball harder before or
since. All I threw were riseballs and they were almost untouchable
that night. When I turned the ball loose, I could see it 'stage.'
It seemed to rise about three times on the way to the plate."

"Other players had similar experiences in their play at various
positions. I don't know if the pro status boosted playing performances or not, but for myself, I could feel a difference."

Besides the league Fincher played in, there have been several
other attempts at making professional softball go, both in fast-
pitch and slow-pitch. One league that hopes to survive is the seven
team International Women's Professional Softball Association. It
has franchises in San Jose, California; Edmonton, Canada; St. Louis,
New York, Buffalo, Philadelphia and Connecticut. One of the most

notable players in the league is Joan Joyce, who is among the best pitchers in the history of women's softball. Joyce is part-owner of the Connecticut Falcons. She is one of the main reasons for the success of the league, and in fact led her team to a fourth consecutive world championship in 1979 as the Falcons defeated the St. Louis Hummers in a best of five series, three games to one. At 5 feet, 10 inches, the 160 pound star has recorded over 650 lifetime wins and has succeeded in keeping her earned run average under 1.00.

Joan Joyce is perhaps the greatest woman player in the history of softball. Her control, variety of pitches, and knowledge of the game make her almost unstoppable on the softball field. (This photograph was taken by Don Grayston and used with the permission of the ASA).

How this particular league does remains to be seen. Perhaps with proper management and a sound financial base, the teams will be able to survive and become leaders for all those who strive to make professional softball a reality.

However if the league does not survive, then the game will simply continue as it has for years with considerable success. For it seems a large number of the softball fans—and players—would like to see the sport remain amateur in nature. This is proven year after year by the large turnout at local games right through national tournament contests.

People enjoy seeing others participating in a sport for the love of the game. Most players have full-time jobs and play softball on weeknights and weekends, sometimes traveling many hours to reach the game site. This is a respected and revered part of the game that cannot be replaced. It is an element any professional league must overcome to win acceptance, and certainly one that must be considered by any group wishing to bring professional softball to the United States in a successful fashion.

On the amateur level in America, there are many prosperous teams in all categories of the game. A good fast-pitch or slow-pitch team can be found in every state. Most communities, in fact, sport several successful teams. Good softball is not hard to find if one takes the time to look. And the price is usually the lowest of any in town. Many times games are simply free of charge. If a person wants to know where the major tournaments are being staged or what nearby towns produce top-notch softball teams, he or she may contact their local recreation department or write to the ASA or ISC. Those addresses are provided following this chapter.

Perhaps only two teams in the United States have made money consistently over the past several years. Those two teams are The King and His Court and The Queen and Her Maids. Both, like the Harlem Globetrotters of basketball fame, travel around the country and into foreign lands playing their distinctive brand of softball against all comers.

Instead of fielding nine players, they feature just four. With a pitcher, catcher, first baseman and shortstop, they regularly beat the teams they face. Not only do they win most games, but do it in a way that entertains everyone in the park.

The King and His Court was started in 1946 by a fellow named Eddie Feigner. Feigner was a pitcher with an excellent reputation.

His four man team started after a barroom discussion in which he was told that his softball ability did not equal that reputation.

Upon hearing this Feigner challenged the outspoken gentleman to bring any nine players to the softball field where he would play them using just three players and himself as pitcher! He explained the minimum of four was needed so that the bases could be loaded with a batter still available. The challenge was accepted and Feigner's team won 7-0. The future King struck out 19 batters in the seven inning contest and pitched himself a perfect game!

After winning the contest, he decided he could make money challenging teams with his four person squad and set out on the road. Since that time, he has pitched thousands of games before droves of softball fans. In his exhibitions, Feigner pitches blindfolded, throws fastballs behind his back, between his legs and from second base.

He has for years demonstrated numerous windups and pitches, all to the delight of the crowd. Feigner has pitched on national television many times, and has advanced the game of softball in parts of the United States and world that have never had the opportunity to witness softball skill such as demonstrated by this great pitcher. Feigner lives in Fallbrook, California and will line up games with teams from virtually any part of America.

The female counterpart to the King and His Court is The Queen and Her Maids. Founded in 1964, the team in led by Rosie Beaird. Beaird and the Maids also travel extensively to play various softball teams. She is a tremendous athlete and utilizes many pitches in attempts to befuddle opponents and entertain the crowds that come to see her pitch and play. Hailing from Rolling Hills Estates, California, the Queen and Her Maids also book games all over the country each year. Rose Beaird, like Feigner, frequently shows up on national television to display her amazing skills.

These two teams and others like them are fine representatives of the game. Both run exhibitions that are fun for the entire family whether anyone has actively participated in softball or not.

Softball is hungry for the adulation and attention it deserves. On television, radio and newspapers across the land, the sport will undoubtedly begin to see more exposure in the future. Due to the increasing numbers in the world playing softball, the media will have to react by providing more coverage of this ever growing sport.

As it stands now, softball players and fans alike are willing to continue supporting softball as they have in the past. They will do this by purchasing equipment, sponsoring teams, building ballparks and buying anything written about the game. Very few sports can claim the same loyalty.

Finally, we can clearly see the sport of softball growing rapidly and in the process entertaining millions each year. These facts alone guarantee the future of softball in America and around the world.

The Guanella's team placed third in the ASA National Tournament in 1979 after finishing fourth in 1978. 1979 proved to be a fine year for the club; in addition to their third place spot in the ASA, they finished fourth in the International Softball Congress tournament. (The ISC is explained in the chapter on the history of softball.)

It is interesting to note that four of the players were named 1979 first team All-Americans. They were Parnow, Marsh, Allena, and Stofflet. K. G. Fincher also made a bid for All-American honors after pitching well in the tournament.

Appendix

Addresses

At this point it would be appropriate to supply you with a comprehensive list of addresses pertaining to softball.

Included will be found the Associations that oversee the game today and three publications that deal exclusively with softball. In addition, you will find manufacturers making softball equipment and uniforms, an umpiring association, a scorebook concern, and an insurance carrier for athletic teams.

The list is not intended as an endorsement of their philosophies or products, but as a helpful addition for those in search of the various products or services rendered by these companies.

ASSOCIATIONS

The Amateur Softball Association of America
2801 N. E. 50th Street
Oklahoma City, Oklahoma 73111

The International Softball Congress
2523 West 14th Street Road
Greeley, Colorado 80631

PUBLICATIONS

Balls and Strikes Newspaper and ASA Magazine
Both official publications of the ASA
2801 N. E. 50th Street
Oklahoma City, Oklahoma 73111

Softball World Newspaper
Post Office Box 10151
Oakland, California 94610

Fastpitch Softball News Bulletin
2835 - 2nd Street
Norco, California 91760

SCORING

Scoremaster Scorebook Co.
Post Office Box 46038
Hollywood, California

UMPIRING

National Federation of ASA Umpires
Post Office Box 11437
Oklahoma City, Oklahoma 73136

PITCHING MACHINES

Sports Equipment, Inc.
Curvemaster Division
Department 0000
Greenville, Illinois 62246

EQUIPMENT MANUFACTURERS

Dudley Sports Equipment
120 Mill Street
Dublin, Pennsylvania 18917

General Sportcraft Co., Ltd.
Bergenfield, New Jersey 07621

Ten Pro Corporation
King Manor Drive
King of Prussia, Pennsylvania 19406

Worth Sports Co.
Tullahoma, Tennessee 37388

Easton-Curley-Bates Co.
860 Stanton Road
Burlingame, California 94010

Wilson Sporting Goods
2233 West Street
River Grove, Illinois 60171

Rawlings Sporting Goods
2300 Delmar Boulevard
St. Louis, Missouri 63166

MacGregor Sporting Goods
25 East Union Avenue
East Rutherford, New Jersey 07073

AMF-Voit
3801 South Harbor Boulevard
Santa Ana, California 92704

Hyde-Spot-Bilt
432 Columbia Street
Cambridge, Massachusetts 02141

H. Harwood and Sons, Inc.
1567 Forrest Avenue
LaGrange, Georgia 30240

Swingster Athletic Apparel
5700 Broadmoor
Mission, Kansas 66202

Southland Athletic Clothing
714 East Grove
Terrell, Texas 75160

Nakona Company
Post Office Box 329
Nocona, Texas 76255

Hillerich and Bradsby Co.
Louisville Slugger Bats
Louisville, Kentucky

INSURANCE

C. W. Bellinger Co.
499 Bloomfield Avenue
Montclair, New Jersey 07042

About the Author

Brian Sobel is a ten-year veteran of the amateur fast pitch wars (he pitches). In addition he is the former news and sports director of KVML and KROG radio in Sonora, California, has edited *Kidsport* magazine, and worked as a sports stringer for the Associated Press.

Index